A NEW CAPSTONE

FOR DECISION MAKING

NEW STRATEGIC MANAGEMENT,
POLITICAL ECONOMY AND LEADERSHIP

Juan Pablo Stegmann, Ph.D.

En Route Books and Media, LLC

Saint Louis, MO

⊕ENROUTE
Make the time

En Route Books and Media, LLC

5705 Rhodes Avenue

St. Louis, MO 63109

Contact us at

contactus@enroutebooksandmedia.com

Cover Credit: Juan Pablo Stegmann

Copyright 2025 Juan Pablo Stegmann

ISBN-13: 979-8-88870-445-5

Library of Congress Control Number:

Available online at https://catalog.loc.gov

Table of Contents

Introduction

Richard Feynman wrote his famous "Lectures on Physics" many years ago. They were revolutionary because they laid out a unified, high-level conceptual view of all physics, incorporating advanced mathematical models. They provided radical rationality, inspired and entertained non-specialists, and were a solid reference source for academia and research.

This book, "A New Capstone," published in two modules: "A New Strategic Management, Political Economy and Leadership" and "Decision Making with Discernment," has a similar purpose: to create a new Capstone, an integrated, simple, unified, high-level version that makes decisions in the best possible way, seeks to be transformative, and builds a more humane world, a better world.

Universities call Capstone the last course that many careers end with. It relies on the discipline of "Strategic Management" (at the left of the image), to integrate career subjects and prepare graduates for decision-making.

This book proposes a new Capstone: decisions are no longer based on very limited strategic management, but on discernment, which, as the image shows, is supported by several columns.

This new Capstone has several characteristics:

1. It integrates, unifies, and simplifies **strategic management and business disciplines** (marketing, operations, human resources, international management, etc.) and incorporates a key competency: "**critical thinking**."

2. It integrates **political economy**, providing crucial insight for society: a nation's success is based on its "**Intellectual Capital**" (knowledge, relationships, innovation, and processes).

3. It integrates it into **leadership**, a leadership based on an organizational process that seeks **excellence and greatness**.

4. It integrates them into a new discipline, **discernment**, for decision-making, incorporating disciplines from **philosophy, cultures, religions, spirituality, psychology, ethics, and social responsibility**. In other words, it **humanizes decision-making, seeking the best for society**.

As the purpose is to provide a decision-making tool, this new Capstone is oriented towards projecting the future. To achieve this, Part 1 presents a tool for analyzing future strategies, Part 2 analyzes the resources needed to build a better future for society, Part 3 presents leadership by process that leads society to a better future. Volume 2 presents discernment as a process for making future-oriented decisions.

Discernment is a key process for making decisions and seeking the best for the future of the person and society. Discernment inspires, enlightens, energizes, humanizes, transforms, heals, and promotes social action. Discernment seeks that the decisions of individuals, organizations, society, nations, lead to constant improvement, to make decisions with wisdom, awareness, transcendence, values, religiosity, community, with meaning, in contact with oneself, seeking transformation, healing, and social action. This helps anyone in their daily lives, parents, children, families, students, professionals, managers, government officials, to make decisions with a human, mature, deep, rational, broad, integrated, unified, simple vision that leads to the common good.

In short, this new Capstone seeks a new mode of decision-making that will best benefit society's future.

Summary

This book is based on solid research, a rich literature review with 500+ authors, and two statistical research papers. For the reader who wants to go to the sources, I invite you to visit my website, https://www.juanpablo-stegmann.net/, where you can find a book titled "Leadership, a journey to world peace", in four volumes, which delves deeper into these topics

Capstone Volume 1, Part 1. Strategic Management.

Part 1 is revolutionary.

Unity, simplicity

Presents a new integrated version of strategic management, ending the atomization and lack of unity of current strategic management. It unifies the models and theories of strategic management into a single model; it integrates business disciplines (marketing, operations, human resources, organizations, international, etc.) with strategic management. On one page we can visualize a set of charts summarizing the recommended strategies of an organization; each chart links the strategies to the ability to create economic value; they link the strategies to each other: for example, whether organizational, human resources and operations strategies are consistent with competitive and growth strategies; shows which theories underpin these strategies by introducing rationality: such theories are contingent on such strategic environments and strategies, and not on others.

Critical thinking

By linking strategic management to the creation of economic value, it incorporates metrics, which help to decide whether strategies are correct, eliminating the vagueness of current strategic management. This allows critical thinking to be developed for each strategy, which is key for decision makers. Critical thinking is a limited tool in the face of the complexities of decision making, leading to the need to incorporate **discernment,** as we will see in Volume 2.

Interdisciplinary thinking

Linking the discipline of strategic management with functional strategies, with political economy, with leadership, and with the disciplines that provide discernment (knowledge management, philosophy, religions, psychology, ethics, and social responsibility) is a powerful source of interdisciplinary thinking, a key competence of all managers.

Excellence and leadership

The metric of economic value creation proposed by corporate finance shows that the success of an organization requires the search for the best, for excellence, for the alternative that produces the best results. This links strategic management with **leadership**, as we will see in Part 3.

Intellectual capital

Linking strategic management with economic value creation allows the development of a financial analysis framework that highlights the **crucial role of resources** for the survival and success of modern organizations, especially Leif Edvinsson's intellectual capital, composed of human, social, renewal and process capital, linking strategic management to the political economy, as discussed in Part 2. Intellectual capital integrates and empowers society, eliminating the debate between individualism versus collectivism. It is also an extraordinary tool for developing discernment in decision making, as shown in Volume 2.

Experiential learning

Part 1 invites the reader to experiential learning: 1. Analyzing a case study based on the well-known Starbucks, 2. Analyzing examples of the 120 largest companies in the United States, and 3. Playing with a financial simulation to understand economic value creation and how it is linked to the organization's reality. In this way, it allows the reader to discover the intuitions presented by their own experience. Volume 2 invites personal exercises to develop each of the ten dimensions of our discernment.

Cutting-edge thinking

Part 1 presents a new version of strategic management that draws on the thinking of five Nobel laureates over the past decades, and on McKinsey's vision of economic value creation and growth strategies, giving it a fundamental intellectual and practical underpinning.

Capstone Volume 1, Part 2. Political Economy.

Part 2 is revolutionary.

Incorporating political economy into the Capstone is crucial for decision-making.

Part 2 ends the sterile debate between left and right and focuses on how a nation should maximize national intellectual capital, promoting economic growth and social justice.

According to Leif Edvinsson, the intellectual capital of a nation or organization is the sum of human capital, social capital, renewal capital, and process capital:

- **Human capital** reflects knowledge, skills, experience, education, competencies, values, health, intuition, motivation, and entrepreneurship.
- **Social capital** reflects the social fabric, values, order, civility, sense of community, reciprocity, goodwill, social behavior, democratic

functioning, respect for laws and institutions, rule of law, civic and political freedoms, internationality, culture of trust, social responsibility, culture of trust.

- **Renewal capital** reflects the capacity for innovation, growth, investment in research and development, and an environment for entrepreneurship.
- **Process capital** reflects production capacity, information technology, management systems, intellectual and structural assets, processes, production, information systems, laboratories, infrastructure, transportation, technology, quality management system, and productivity.

Capstone Volume 1, Part 3. Leadership.

Part 3 is revolutionary.

Part 3 shows how leaders maximize the intellectual capital of organizations and nations, and Volume 2 presents a statistical analysis showing how a leadership culture, as proposed in this book, has better social outcomes than individualistic and collectivistic cultures.

Part 1 shows how successful organizations require excellence. Incorporating leadership and excellence is crucial for decision-making.

It presents a new conception of leadership as a process, enriched by the Baldrige Excellence Framework, its values, and its structure to promote great leadership, to produce the best results for society, as shown in Parts 1, 2, and 4.

Capstone Volume 2. Discernment.

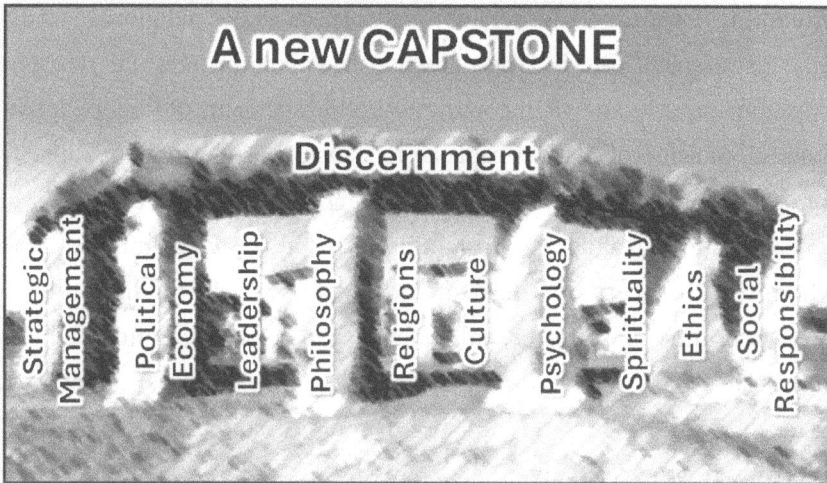

Volume 2 of this book, *A New Capstone for Decision Making: Discernment*, is revolutionary.

Discernment is the heart of the Capstone: it integrates, unites, and perfects Parts 1, strategic management, 2, political economy, and 3, leadership. This integration of knowledge, this unity in decision making, this simplification in our decision making, is revolutionary.

However, the most important aspect about Volume 2 is the richness and humanism that discernment generates.

Universities and the world of organizations advocate critical thinking for decision making. Critical thinking is a skill, an intellectual, systemic exercise that links the environment, strategies, and results. The results are supported by metrics that determine whether a decision is correct.

Discernment is a richer, more human competency that incorporates the whole person and the community in decision-making.

Discernment incorporates our capacity for reflection, meditation, contemplation, and our conscience. This improves our lives because it strengthens our capacity to appreciate and create transcendence (goodness, beauty, truth), pillars of our happiness; it incorporates our higher values, which are engines of personal and social transformation, leading to love, promoting a culture of leadership; it incorporates our religiosity, which leads us to collaborate in God's creation task; incorporates our relationships, our capacity to live in community, building teams of leaders; incorporates our sense of life, our capacity to transform suffering, our capacity for psychological introspection to understand our decisions, our power of transformation, healing and promotion of social action, forming citizens who vote with discernment, leaders who have the capacity for discernment.

Discernment inspires us, enlightens us, energizes us, unites us, heals us, transforms us, in other words, makes us leaders. Our discernment leads us to a better, simpler world that fills our souls, teaches us how to live, and integrates us as persons and as a society.

Making decisions with discernment humanizes society, integrates it, helps to solve strategic, ethical, and social dilemmas, towards happiness, towards a better world, towards a peaceful world.

Competencies Provided by this Book

This book provides the six categories of competencies proposed by Fink's taxonomy of "Meaningful Learning", which are crucial for every person, citizen, professional, manager, government member, and for the whole society. This taxonomy is used by accrediting bodies of university programs, as it enriches Bloom's taxonomy. Fink's taxonomy promotes holistic, transformative learning, emphasizing the human dimension, and continuous learning.

1. Foundational knowledge.

The book provides knowledge of disciplines that everyone should know: strategic management, political economy, leadership, and discernment.

2. Skills.

The book promotes:

- Critical thinking and discernment for decision making.
- Interdisciplinary thinking.
- Creative thinking.

3. Integration.

The interdisciplinary thinking framework proposed in this book seeks to relate ideas, people, and areas of life. It seeks to create organizational knowledge in both personal and work environments. It seeks the integration of the individual and society, promoting discernment for complex decision making, linking the environment, decisions, and results.

4. Human dimension.

The book helps each person to know himself/herself better, to make decisions without our subjectivity distorting those decisions; it seeks to achieve happiness; it seeks to help each person to know society better, to interact in a positive way seeking the common good; it seeks to promote leadership and social responsibility. It seeks to facilitate a dialogue between global cultures, between religions, learning from the richness that diversity brings.

5. Common good, peace, and social harmony.

This book presents how discernment energizes, inspires, and drives us to promote the common good.

6. Innovation and creativity.

This book presents how discernment illuminates, inspires, energizes, creates, transforms, vitalizes, and heals.

Part 1

A New Strategic Management

Introduction

In the last decades, several economists, including 5 Nobel Prize winners[1] created a new version of strategic management[2] to analyze the causal relationship between environments, strategies, and outcomes, introducing economic modeling, metrics, and some advanced economic theories, such as game theory and the resource-based view of the firm, to analyze strategic management decisions.

Michael Porter's *Competitive Strategies* and *Competitive Advantage* pioneered this approach, followed by works such as Jean Tirole's *The Theory of Industrial Organization*, Oz Shy's *Industrial Organization*, Stephen Martin's *Advanced Industrial Economics*, Avinash K. Dixit and Barry J. Nalebuff's *Thinking Strategically*, David Besanko and David Dranove's *Economics of Strategy*.

This new version of strategic management has a strong affinity with what our common sense tells us. In our daily and professional lives, our common sense tells us that when we make a decision that involves

---

[1] Ronald Coase (1991), John Forbes Nash (1994), Oliver E. Williamson (2009), Jean Tirole (2014) and Oliver Hart (2016).

[2] Michael Porter's Competitive Strategies and Competitive Advantage pioneered this approach, followed by works such as The Theory of Industrial Organization by Jean Tirole, Industrial Organization by Oz Shy, Advanced Industrial Economics by Stephen Martin, Thinking Strategically by Avinash K. Dixit and Barry J. Nalebuff, Economics of Strategy by David Besanko and David Dranove.

choosing among several alternatives, we go for the one that produces the best results, with the least effort.

Corporate finance calls this phenomenon "**economic value creation**": when we invest in the best alternatives, we create economic value.

McKinsey, the prestigious management consulting firm, developed a financial model, the EVA$^{(TM)}$ model (Economic Value Added), which supports such intuition and allows us to understand in depth what economic value creation consists of.

Incorporating the EVA metric in strategic management allows us to know if certain strategies help to create economic value, and it allows us to model all strategic decisions by analyzing their capacity to create economic value.

This gives rise to a new strategic management: we can integrate all general strategies (competitive, innovation and resource strategies), functional strategies (marketing, operations, human resources, organizations, planning, international strategies, corporate strategies), other strategic management models (Business Model, SWOT, PESTLE, Blue Ocean, BCG, GE/McKinsey, Miles and Snow) and the strategic management theories that support them.

This new version of strategic management brings clarity of ideas, simplicity, integration of knowledge, rationality, critical thinking, practicality, allows incorporating the social dimension of strategic management, allows analyzing the strategies of non-business organizations, non-profit organizations, communities, governments, NGOs, armed forces, clubs, churches and other agents, which has a key value for managers who must understand the entire organization and visualize the future.

Chapter 1

The Link between Economic Value Creation, Strategic Environment, Strategies, and Results

At the heart of this new strategic management is the ability of strategies to create economic value. The EVA™ Model[1] developed by Bennet Stewart[2] and Tom Copeland[3] (McKinsey & Company Inc.) measures the economic value creation of an organization.[4] The EVA model involves three variables

---

[1] The EVA model [EVA = net operating profit after tax - (invested capital x weighted average cost of capital)] leads to exactly the same value as the DCF [PV = CF1 / (1+r) + CF2 / (1+r)2 + ... [T / (k - r)] / (1+r)n-1 meaning: PV = present value; CFi = cash flow in year I; n = number of periods; r = discount rate; T = terminal year cash flow; g expected growth rate].

[2] Stewart, G. Bennett. *The Quest for Value: A Guide for Senior Managers.* New York. HarperCollins. 1999.

[3] Copeland, Tom, et al. *Valuation: Measuring and Managing the Value of Companies.* 3rd edition. McKinsey & Company Inc. John Wiley & Sons, Inc. 2000.

[4] Financial science has developed mathematical models to measure economic value creation. Discounted cash flow is the most popular: it measures how much money the company will earn in the future, so the value of the company today is the net present value of future cash flows. Before making any investment, investors analyze the risks and outcomes of potential stocks, and for each level of risk, the investor will invest in the most profitable stock. This logic is reflected in the EVA model.

Economic profit = net operating profit after tax - (invested capital x weighted average cost of capital) leads to exactly the same value as the DCF [PV = CF1 / (1+r) + CF2 / (1+r)2 +.... [T / (k - r)] / (1+r)n-1 which means:

that make it possible to link an organization's strategies with its results, in terms of economic value creation. On the website https://www.juanpablo-stegmann.net/ the reader can find several research papers, books and doctoral theses[5] that explain the statistical foundation linking economic value

PV = present value; CFi = cash flow in year I; n = number of periods; r = discount rate; T = last year's cash flow; g = expected growth rate].

Excerpted from: McKinsey & Company; Tim Koller, Marc Goedhart and David Wessels. *Valuation: Measuring and Managing the Value of Companies*. Hoboken, N.J. John Wiley & Sons. 2000.

[5] Stegmann, Juan Pablo. *Using the EVA model for corporate stock investment; impact of knowledge, growth and monopoly power on economic value. An investigation of 168 U.S. firms*. Doctoral dissertation. Poland. University of Warsaw. 2005.

- *An integrative and modern approach to Business Strategy and Entrepreneurship based on Value Based Management and Knowledge Management. Becoming a learning organization*. Doctoral dissertation. California. Pacific Western University. 2001.

- An Integrated View of Strategic Management" in *The Journal of Interdisciplinary Economics* 18 (2077): 275-302.

- Towards an integrated strategic management" in *The Journal of Interdisciplinary Economics* 18 (2007): 35-69.

- *Strategic Value Management. Economic value Creation and the Management of the Firm*. Hoboken, N. J. John Wiley and Sons. 2009.

- *Modern Business Strategy. How to grow, modernize, internationalize and compete successfully in the new environment*. IEEC. 2002.

- *Modern strategic management*. IEEC. 2000.Argentina.

- Strategic Value Management. A new generation of strategic management thinking", annual conference at the Strategic Management Society. Rome. 2010.

- *The foundations of Strategic Management: Relationship between Growth, Economic Value Creation, Knowledge Creation and Monopoly Power*. Atlanta. Academy of International Business. 2002.

creation, with strategic environments, strategies, and results, based on the EVA metric. These papers demonstrate five hypotheses[6] that provide metrics and an analytical framework for connecting strategic management and economic value creation. Two of these hypotheses are fundamental: 1) market power and economic profits are positively correlated and 2) knowledge and sales growth are positively correlated.

- *Towards an Interdisciplinary View of Business Ethics*. Vermont. Norwich University. 2011.

- Personal Values Versus Stock Value Maximization. Conflicts and Solutions", annual conference at the Academy of Management. Montreal. 2010.

- Strategic management and value" in *Cámara de Comercio Ecuatoriana Americana*. Quito. 2010.

- An integrative approach to Modern Strategy, based in Value Based and Knowledge" lecture at the Third International Research Seminar of Coggin College of Business, University of North Florida / Centre for Europe, Warsaw University. Jacksonville. 2003.

- *The foundations of Strategic Management: Relationship between Growth, Economic Value Creation, Knowledge Creation and Monopoly Power*. Academy of International Business. Atlanta. 2002.

- *An integrative and modern approach to business strategy and entrepreneurship, based on Value Based Management and Knowledge Management*, lecture at the Second Coggin College of Business International Research Seminar, University of North Florida / Centre for Europe, Warsaw University. Jacksonville. 2002.

[6] Economic performance and growth are not correlated.

Hypothesis 2. Growth and knowledge are positively correlated.

Hypothesis 3. Economic performance and knowledge are not correlated.

Hypothesis 4. Market power and economic performance are positively correlated.

Economic performance and growth are negatively correlated for different levels of knowledge.

1. **Economic benefits (EVA) depend on the success of competitive strategies.**

EVA measures the economic benefits of the company's profitability above the profitability of other companies. For example, if my company's profitability is 10%, but the profitability of other similar companies is 15%, my EVA will be negative, minus 5%, I am destroying 5% of economic value in the period.

If an organization has a negative EVA, the more money it invests, the more its economic value falls. If it has a negative EVA, it cannot justify new investments and growth projects, so it is not easy for it to grow, and in case it decides to do so, it is not easy to get investors, so the company will have to resort to its self-generated funds, which may be limited.

This is fundamental; an organization must first ensure its profitability. It is like the lifeblood of an organization, what keeps it alive. This concurs with our common sense: invest in the best.

One might say: EVA brings me nothing new. But it doesn't. EVA makes it possible to measure economic value creation and link results to environments and strategies.

For decades, economic science has linked profitability to the level of competition. EVA goes a step further and measures the level of competitiveness: if my profitability is higher than others, I am more competitive than they are, and my competitive strategies are the way to achieve it. And the heart of the competitive strategy depends on the organization having better resources than others, which we can also measure in terms of intellectual capital (knowledge, relationships, capacity to innovate, and processes).

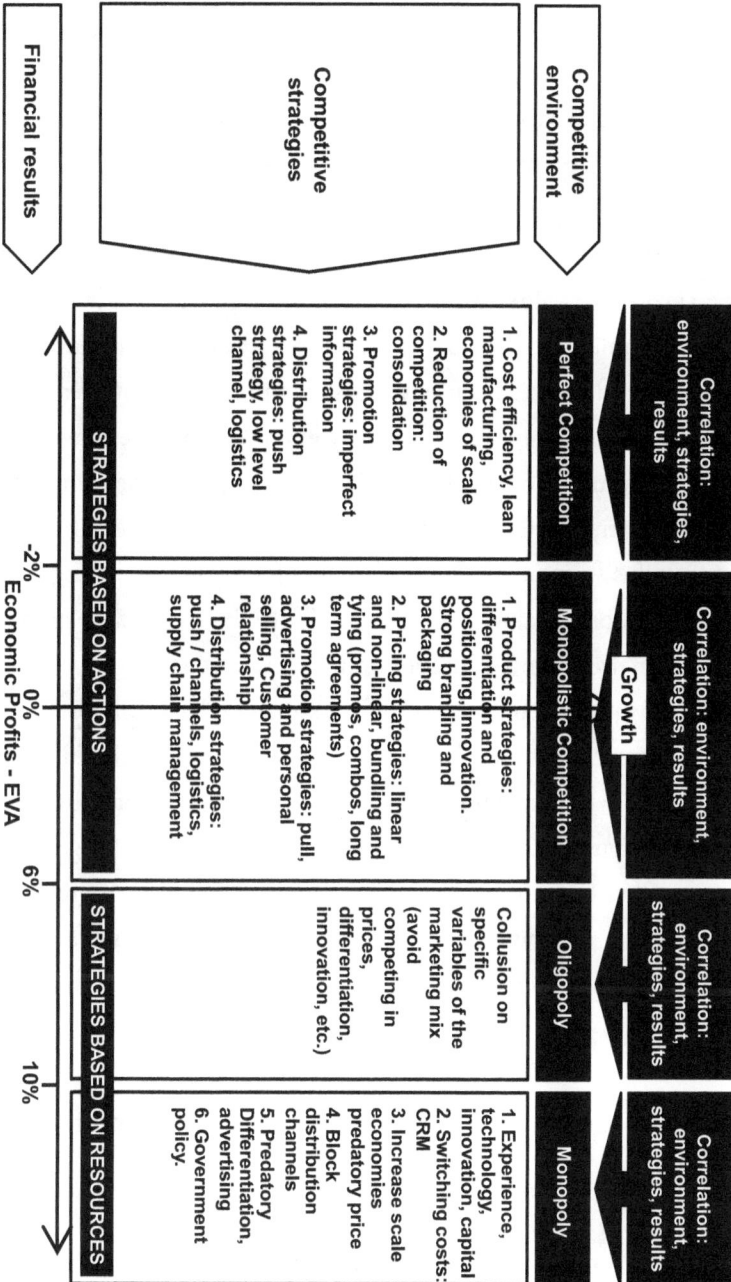

Figure 1. Correlation between competitive environment, competitive strategies, and economic results (EVA)

Figure 1 shows how the EVA model allows framing the correlation between competitive environments, competitive strategies, and economic benefits. The graph shows how certain competitive environments promote certain competitive strategies and create or destroy economic value. On the left of the graph, perfect competition environments promote low-cost competitive strategies, and in general have a negative EVA, below -2%, destroying economic value; in the middle of the graph, monopolistic competition environments promote differentiation strategies, and have an EVA between -2% and +6%. Both environments promote strategies based on actions, which the competition can copy, and therefore, they have a limited capacity to promote positive EVAs, higher returns than the competition.

A little further to the right of the graph, the oligopoly environment allows for collusive strategies where companies avoid competing, creating sustained economic value above 6%; finally, to the right of the graph, monopolistic environments promote unique resource strategies, with EVAs above 10%. Both environments promote strategies based on unique, inimitable resources, which the competition cannot easily copy, and hence their greater capacity to create positive EVAs, higher returns than the competition. This is crucial. Competitive environments impact all organizational strategies. Environments and strategies make it possible to create or destroy economic value and have positive or negative EVAs, which is crucial for an organization's success or survival.

Appendix 3 explains this chart in detail.

2. Sales growth depends on the success of growth and innovation strategies.

To create economic value, companies need to grow sales based on innovation strategies (new products, customers, markets, businesses, and channels).

Figure 2 shows how growth and innovation strategies can create or destroy economic value. On the left side of the graph, negative EVA leads to the fact that the more a company grows, the more economic value it destroys, while on the right side of the graph, with positive EVA, the more it grows, the more economic value it creates. The resource-based growth strategies at the top of the chart can create economic value sustainably, but the action-based strategies at the bottom have limited ability to create economic value.

This chart helps to generate critical thinking: not all innovation and growth strategies are beneficial.

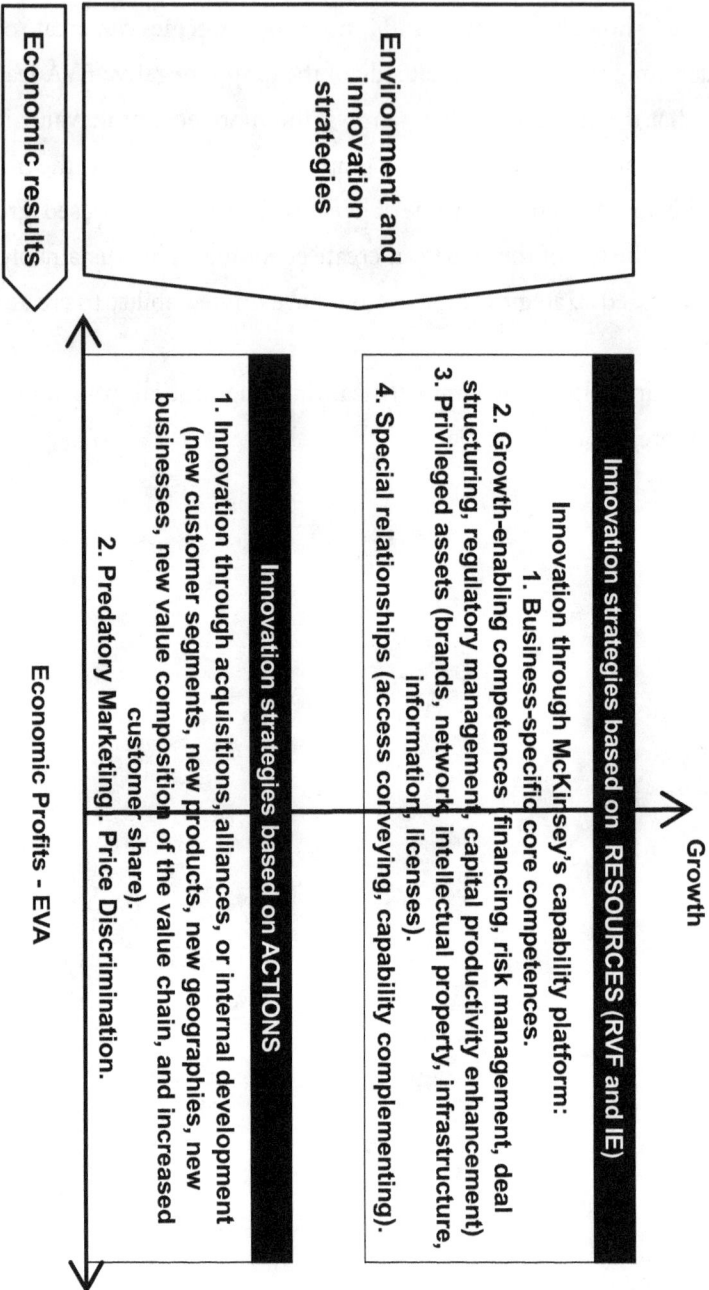

Economic results

Environment and innovation strategies

Growth

Innovation strategies based on RESOURCES (RVF and IE)

Innovation through McKinsey's capability platform:

1. Business-specific core competences.

2. Growth-enabling competences (financing, risk management, deal structuring, regulatory management, capital productivity enhancement)

3. Privileged assets (brands, networks, intellectual property, infrastructure, information, licenses).

4. Special relationships (access conveying, capability complementing).

Innovation strategies based on ACTIONS

1. Innovation through acquisitions, alliances, or internal development (new customer segments, new products, new geographies, new businesses, new value composition of the value chain, and increased customer share).

2. Predatory Marketing. Price Discrimination.

Economic Profits - EVA

Figure 2. Correlation between innovation strategies and sales growth.

This is crucial. The size of an organization can impact its success: it allows it to have better resources, economies of scale, which lower its costs, market power, and greater ability to succeed with innovation. If my competition outgrows me, it is very possible that my business will not be able to survive in the future.

Appendix 3 explains this chart in detail.

3. Intellectual capital (market value of the organization above its book value) depends on the success of resource strategies.

The market value of a company is equal to the initial capital invested, its physical capital, plus the economic value that the company is capable of generating throughout its life, its Market Value Added[7] (MVA).

According to the EVA model, the MVA = present value of future EVAs.

The MVA reflects the future, what investors are willing to pay for the company above its book value, based on the expectation that the company can generate positive economic returns and growth in the future.

That future is based on its resources, intellectual capital, which is measured by the difference between the market value of the organization and its physical capital (in terms of its book value). According to Leif Edvinsson, intellectual capital reflects **human capital** (knowledge), **social capital** (relationships), **renewal capital** (innovation), and **process capital** (equipment and technology). Part 2 of this book analyzes and elaborates on these four capitals, based on the thinking proposed in political economy

---

[7] McKinsey formulates the MVA with the following equation, which provides very interesting data: (Economic profit T+1 / WACC) + NOPLAT T+1 * (Growth g / ROIC) * (ROIC - WACC) / [WACC * (WACC - Growth g)].

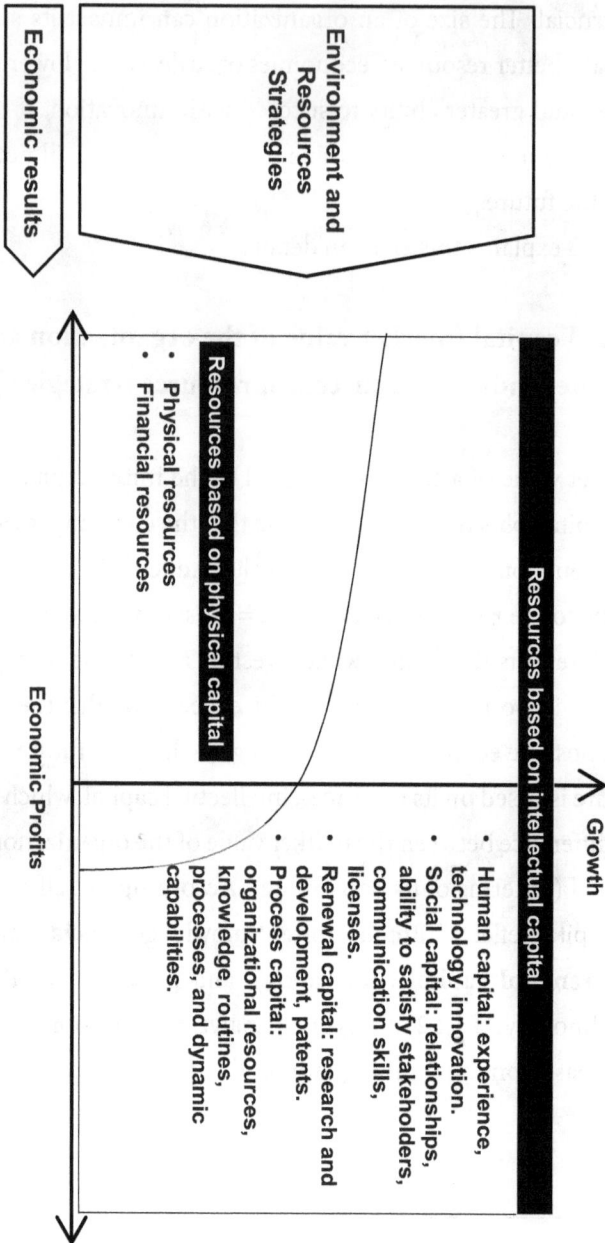

**Figure 3. Correlation between resourcing strategies,
EVA, and sales growth.**

The MVA, the intellectual capital, is the most significant part of the market value of modern organizations. For example, Microsoft's market value is $300 billion; its physical capital is $30 billion; its intellectual capital, its MVA, is $270 billion. Why is MVA, intellectual capital, so high? Because Microsoft is a company based on human capital (knowledge), social capital (relationships), renewal capital (innovation) and process capital (technology), and not so much on physical capital.

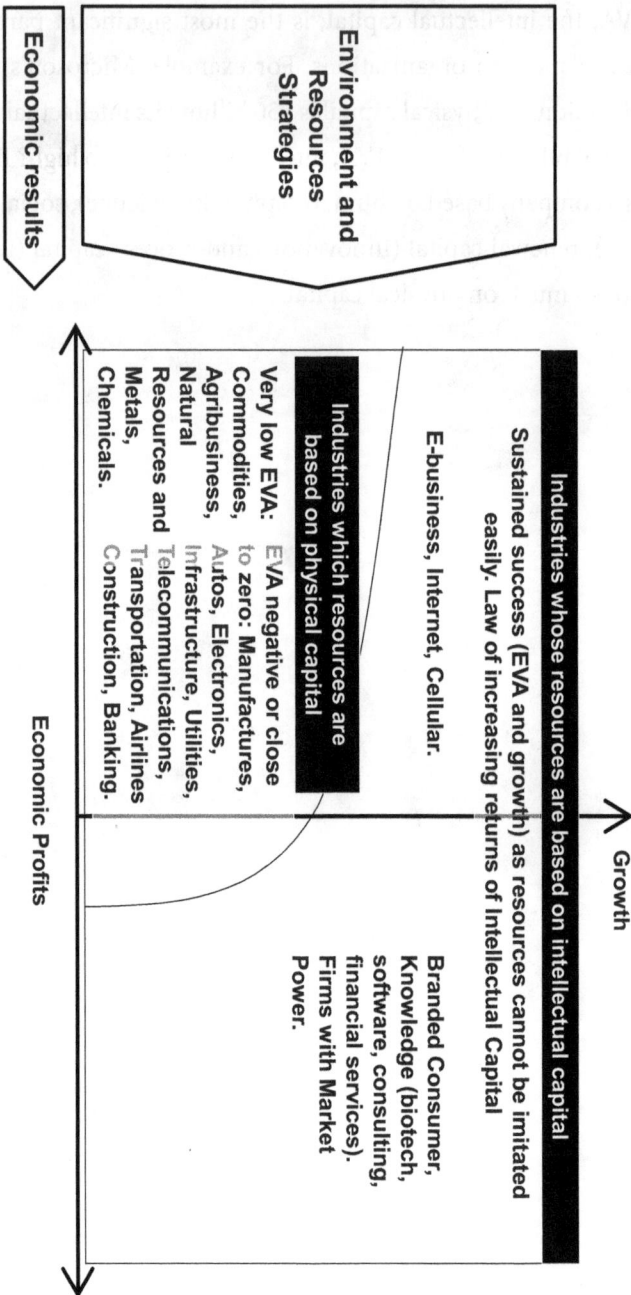

Figure 4. Economic value creation and resources, by industry.

As Figure 4 shows, some industries require large amounts of physical capital, others require large amounts of intellectual capital.

According to Leif Edvinsson, physical capital has several problems: investments in physical capital follow the law of diminishing returns (the more it is invested, the less profit it produces), it wears out and deteriorates. Intellectual capital follows the law of increasing returns: it can grow indefinitely with investment. When Rover and Honda entered a strategic alliance a few decades ago, Honda acquired Rover's intellectual capital, knowledge, and relationships in the Western market, which has grown ever since.

Physical capital can be easily imitated leading the industry to perfect competition. The opposite occurs if the industry is based on intellectual capital.

Intellectual capital can reproduce itself without new investments (the direct cost of producing a new Microsoft Windows that sells online is negligible compared to its sale price, while the direct cost of producing a ton of steel, with high physical capital, is very close to its price). Intellectual capital does not wear out, rust, or deteriorate like physical capital.

Chapter 2

Experiential Learning.
The Strategies of a Company on a Page.

The best way to learn these topics is through personal experience, so throughout this book, we will do experiential learning exercises.

The first exercise will help us understand the relationship between strategic environments - strategies - results in terms of economic value creation.

In this first experiential learning, we will analyze the strategies of a company we all know: Starbucks.

The Starbucks financial data presented below is derived from the financial websites and methodologies explained in Appendix 1. My website https://www.juanpablostegmann.net/ has a database with this data.

The analysis and suggested strategies are based on my opinion and are in no way intended to reflect Starbucks' strategies.

Competitive strategies. Starbucks EVA: 11%.

Starbucks' average annual EVA over the last decade has been 11% per year.

Figure 5 summarizes Starbucks' competitive strategies.

An EVA of 11% indicates that Starbucks is 11% more profitable than similar companies, and therefore either operates in a low competitive environment or is more competitive than its competitors.

Figure 5 indicates that Starbucks operates in a monopolistically competitive environment. The recommended strategies for this environment are strong differentiation, customer satisfaction, excellent quality, variety, service quality, ambience, speed of service, branding, locations, advertising, social media, relationships, consumer education, and music. We will analyze both environments and strategies below.

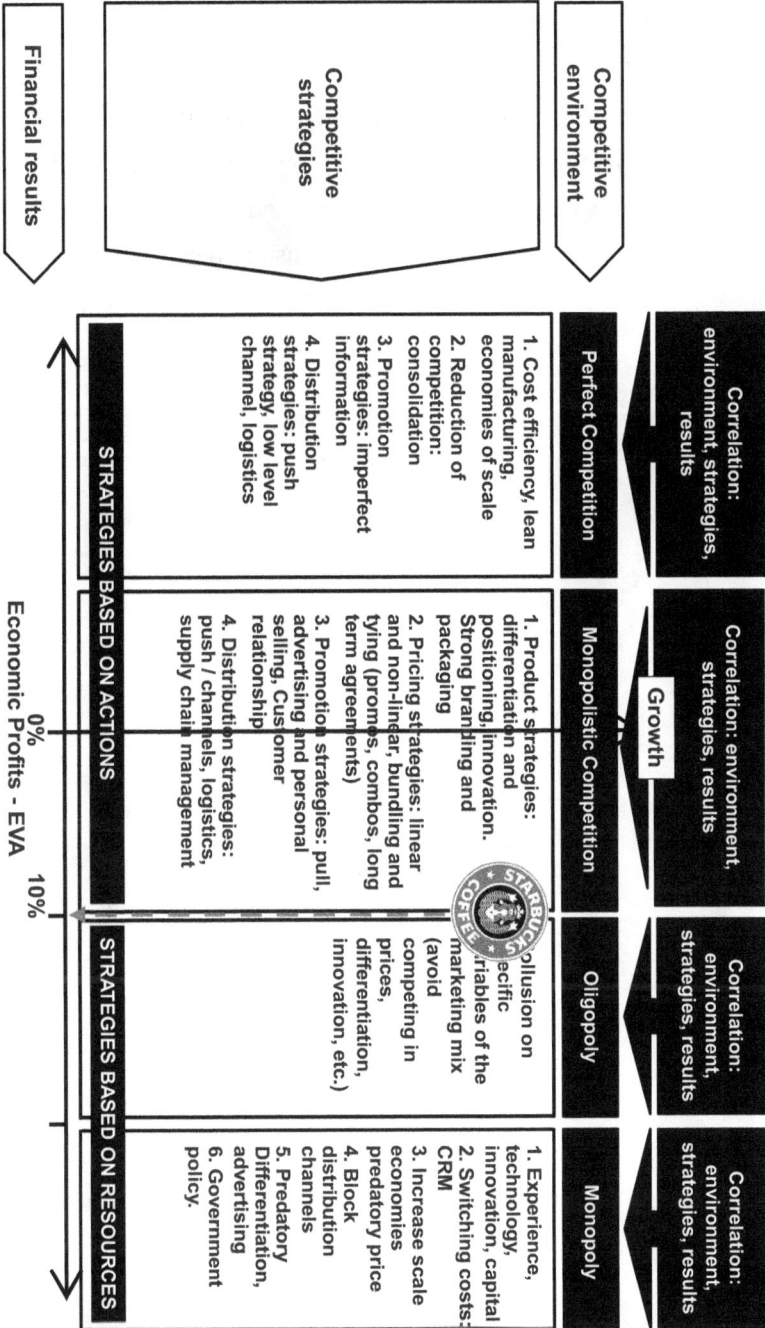

Figure 5. Starbucks. EVA and competitive strategies.

Growth and innovation strategies. Starbucks sales growth: 6%.

Starbucks' average sales growth over the last decade has been 6%.

As Figure 5 shows, 6% is moderate growth, reflecting its innovation strategies based mainly on actions: new restaurants, new geographies, new channels, new products, international expansion, new partners, and new alliances.

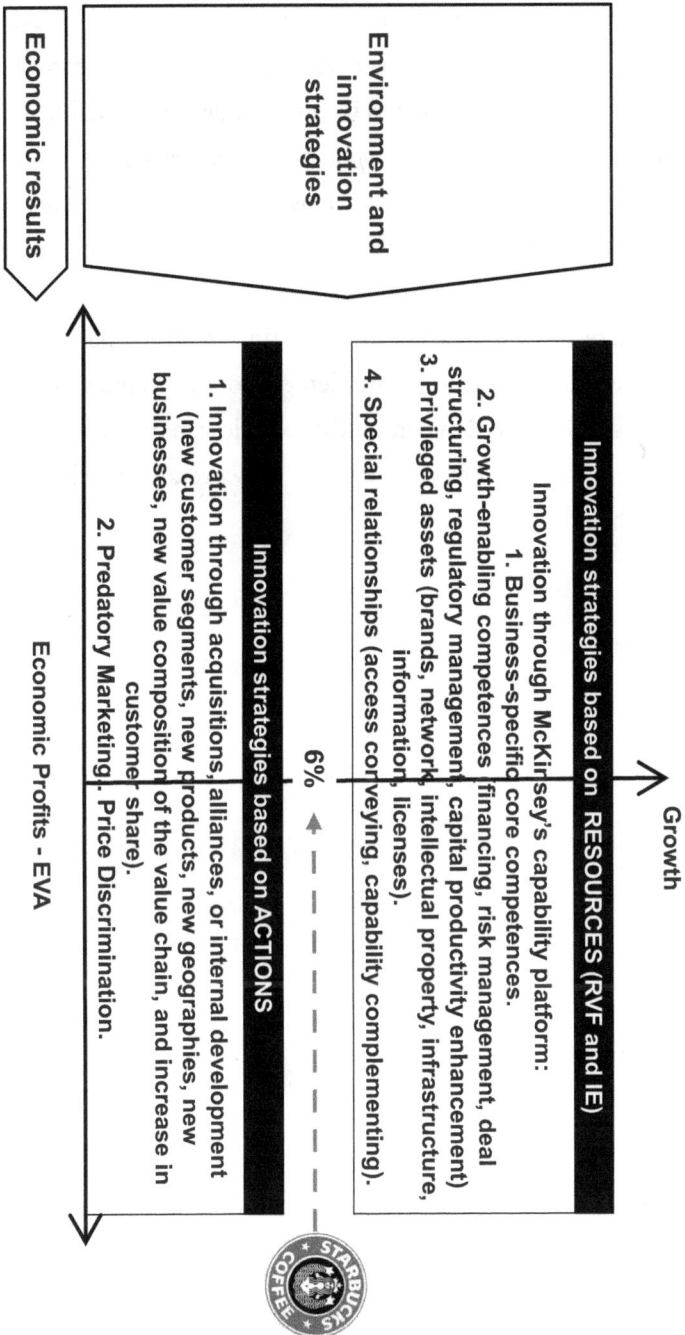

Figure 6. Starbucks. Growth and innovation strategies.

Resource strategies. Starbucks' intellectual capital: 2.2x.

Starbucks' intellectual capital is currently 2.2x, which means that the company's market value is 2.2 times its book value, also called its physical capital, and that difference measures its intellectual capital.

Figure 6 shows that this reflects a reasonable capacity to create intellectual capital: knowledge, relationships, innovation, and process capability.

This is interesting because the first intuition we might have is that any coffee producer should be in the lower left part of the graph, since coffee is part of agribusiness, coffee is a commodity with low margins, with very low intellectual capital (high physical capital). However, Starbucks is on the right side of the graph.

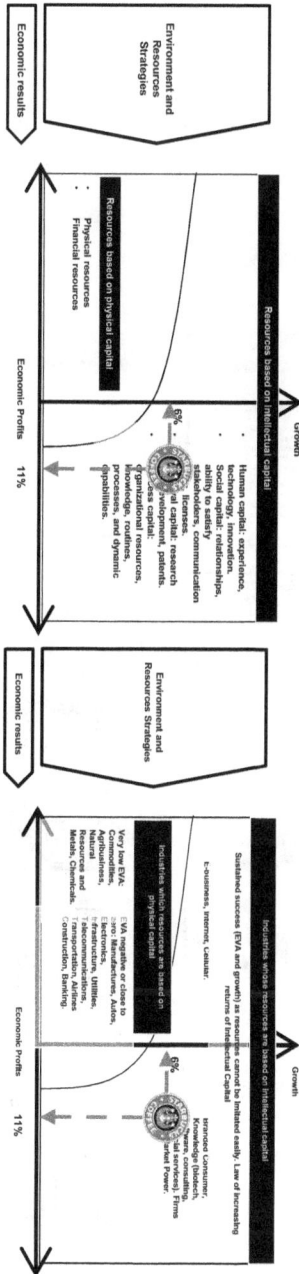

Figure 7. Starbucks resources strategies versus the coffee industry.

Starbucks, functional strategies.

Once we position Starbucks in the EVA model, and agree on its general, competitive, growth and resource strategies, we can position it in the charts for other functional strategies, as shown in Figure 8, based on the models explained in Appendix 3.

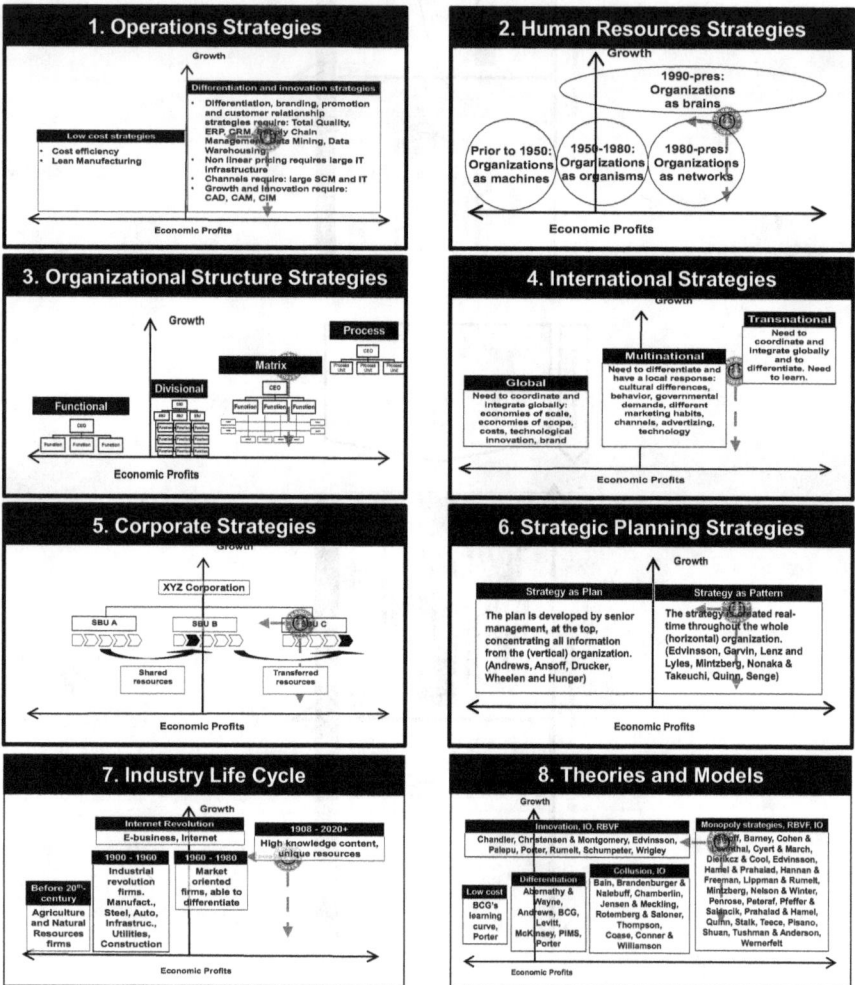

Figure 8. Starbucks. Functional strategies, life cycle and strategic management theories.

Operations strategies are aligned with differentiation, branding, promotion and customer relationship strategies, which require Total Quality, ERP, CRM, supply chain management, data mining, data warehousing and data warehousing initiatives. Channels require great SCM and IT.

Human resources strategies are on the right side of the graph, which may indicate what strategies can be applied in different parts of the organization: organizations as predictable, routine, efficient machines in **operations**; organizations as sensitive organizations that listen, observe, and relate to **customers and suppliers**; organizations as networks in **corporate** issues, linking with suppliers of inputs such as coffee and food; organizations as brains in areas linked to **growth and innovation**, new products, new channels, new regions, etc.

The reader can continue the analysis by referring to Appendix 3, at the end of the book, which analyzes each of these strategies in detail.

Conclusions

In a few minutes, we have learned a cutting-edge version of strategic management, we have been able to analyze the strategic reality of Starbucks, its strategic environment, its possible strategies, and its results. We were able to unify and simplify all strategic management and functional strategies. We have developed critical thinking and interdisciplinary thinking, two key competencies of every manager, to question the different strategies, to see if they help to create economic value, and to see if they are coherent with each other.

This exercise helps us realize that it is not enough to do things right: to create economic value, any organization needs to have a positive EVA, to be more profitable than the competition, and to do so, it needs to have successful competitive strategies, to do better than others.

To create economic value, any organization needs to grow more than the competition and, to do so, it needs to have successful innovation strategies, to do better than others.

It is not enough to have good resources; to create economic value, any organization needs to have intellectual capital, knowledge, and relationships, unique resources, better than the others, and for this, it needs successful resource strategies. If a company has negative economic benefits (EVA), the more the company invests, the more economic value it destroys. This situation affects about 50% of companies, as economic profits compare their profits with the average profits of similar companies.

Chapter 3

Experiential Learning.
Analyzing Business Segments.

A crucial intuition in strategic management is the separation between results because of the strategic environment versus results because of the company's strategies. This makes it possible to analyze business segments, with strategic environments common to the companies in the segment, separating those companies that, due to their strategies, have different results from the segment.

For example, the automotive segment has an average EVA of -2%, while Tesla has an EVA of +11% due to its strategies.

In this exercise we will link two realities: on the one hand, we will visualize the economic value creation of the 120 most recognized companies in the United States; on the other hand, we will analyze what could, in our opinion, be their possible strategic environments and strategies: today, with the help of Artificial Intelligence, it is very easy to investigate their environments, strategies and results.

Appendix 1 presents the methodology to calculate the three core variables of economic value creation for these 120 companies: **EVA** (reflects the results of their competitive strategies), **sales growth** (reflects the results of their innovation strategies) and **intellectual capital** (reflects the results of their resource strategies).

On the website https://www.juanpablostegmann.net/ the reader can find the Excel file with the data and graphs used in the following examples.

Table 1 consolidates these results according to the business segments in which these 120 companies operate:

Table 1. Economic value creation of 120 leading companies, consolidated by segment.

Business Segments	EVA	Sales Growth % (10 years)	Intellectual Capital
Energy	1%	1%	2.06
Steel, minerals	-3%	0%	-0.03
Utilities	-2%	1%	1.46
Manufactures	2%	8%	4.71
Aerospace y defense	-1%	0%	5.63
Transportation	-6%	6%	2.22
Communications, logistics	-1%	7%	7.67
Mass Consumption	11%	0%	22.77
Retail	12%	5%	38.62
Leisure	16%	11%	9.46
Health	6%	6%	12.79
ICT	16%	8%	11.23
Software	6%	15%	15.81

In the following examples, we will only use the first two variables, EVA and sales growth. For two reasons, we will not plot the third variable, intellectual capital.

First, intellectual capital is a consequence of EVA and sales growth, so knowing these two indicators, we can assume intellectual capital. This can be confirmed by looking at the three columns of Table 1, where intellectual capital correlates with EVA and sales growth.

Second, as the graphs above show, the horizontal axis measures EVA and the vertical axis measures sales growth; adding a third variable would require three-dimensional graphs, which are very difficult to read.

Value creation and strategies

The first seven segments in the list (energy, steel, minerals, utilities, manufacturing, aerospace, defense, transportation, telecommunications, logistics) have very low or negative EVAs, between -6% and 2%. These segments require large investments in physical assets, which is reflected in the third column: low intellectual capital.

The "manufacturing" segment has intellectual capital of 4.7x, which is high, which seems contradictory because, in general, these are businesses with a lot of physical capital. This is due to Tesla, which has a very high intellectual capital of 16x (the market value of the share is 16 times its book value), much higher than the rest, which raises the average for the segment.

Something similar happens in the "Aerospace and defense" segment, where Lockheed has an intellectual capital of 14x, much higher than the rest of the companies in the segment, distorting the sample.

The following segments (mass consumption, retail, leisure, health, information technology, software) have high average EVAs. The intellectual capital column explains this good performance: most of them are businesses with a higher intellectual capital component, which allows them to operate with low competition (EVAs close to 10%) and higher growth (average 6%).

In some cases, intellectual capital values are artificially high because some companies have undertaken share buybacks, which raise their market value and reduce the book value of their physical assets.

Analyzing the strategic environment versus a company's strategies

We continue with our experiential learning, incorporating the above-mentioned EVA graph. We will see business segments to separate the strategic environment from the strategies of the companies, especially to visualize how some companies, based on their strategies, managed to have better performances than those of the segment.

Energy, steel, materials, utilities

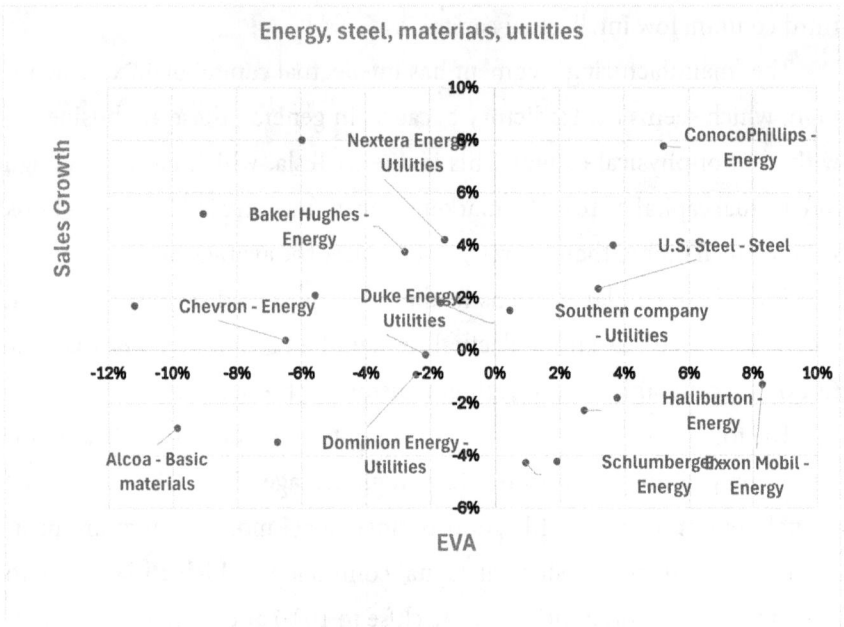

Figure 9. Economic value creation, energy, steel, materials, utilities segments.

These segments have low growth and low EVA, which is to be expected in a mature industry that sells products characterized as commodities, making it difficult for companies in the sector to implement strategies that differentiate them, which leads to intense competition, with low or negative EVAs.

Manufacturing, aerospace, defense

Manufacturers, aerospace, defense

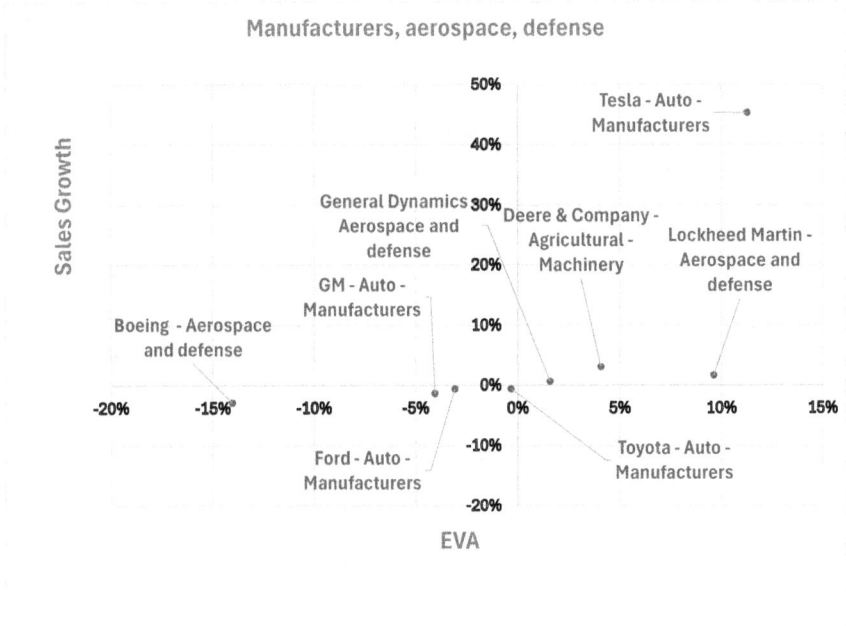

Figure 10. Economic value creation, manufacturing, aerospace, and defense segments.

These segments also have a significant physical capital component; however, they can create intellectual capital so that EVA can be low to moderate. A couple of companies, such as Tesla and Lockheed, have achieved strategies that separate them from the pack, and they can differentiate and innovate.

Transportation, communications and logistics

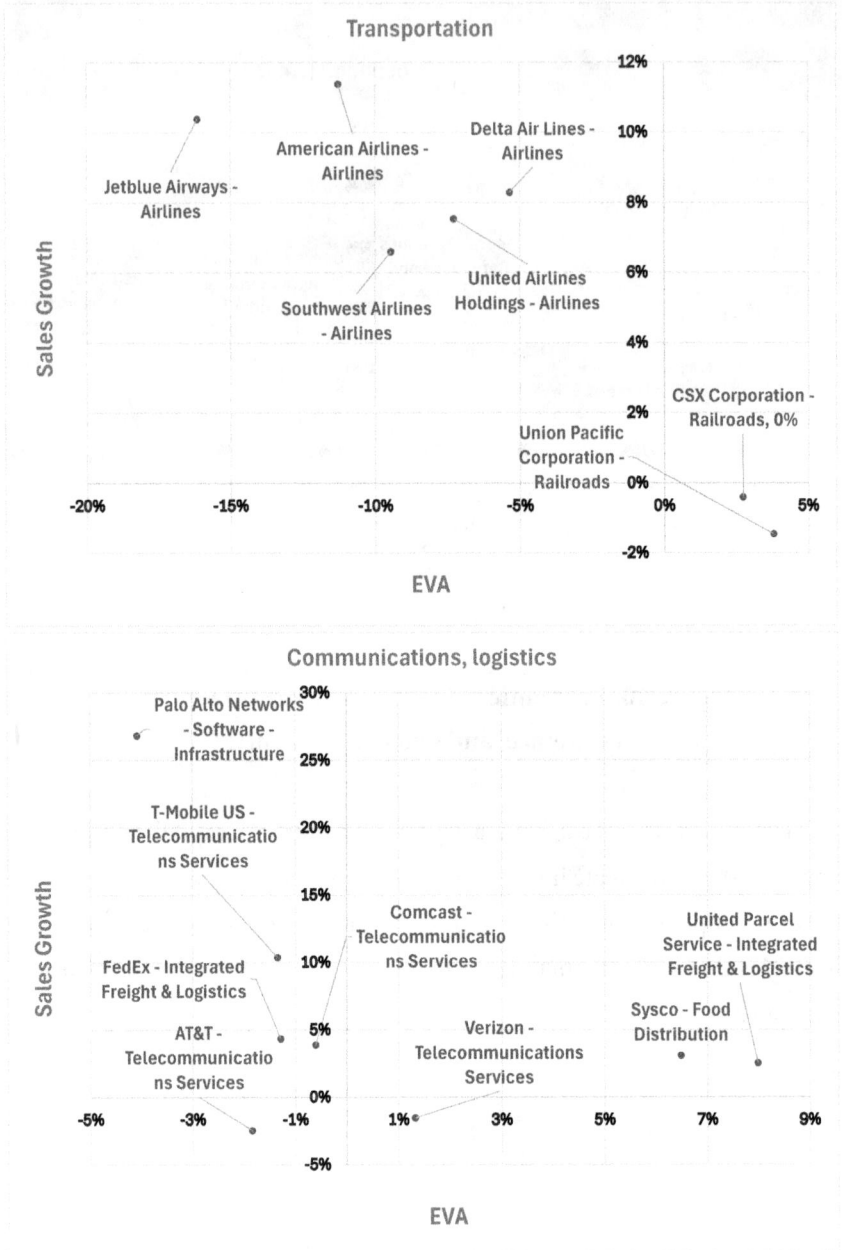

Transportation

Communications, logistics

Figure 11. Economic value creation, transportation, communications, and logistics segments.

In the transportation and communications segments, companies provide standardized services, so they operate with a lot of competition and have low or negative EVAs. Based on their strategies, it is not easy for companies to outperform the segment.

The logistics segment can develop its own services with sophisticated systems, with a little more intellectual capital.

An important conclusion can be drawn. The lower the intellectual capital, i.e., the organization's resources, the lower its ability to differentiate and innovate. It can be automatically concluded that businesses with a lot of physical capital, not only the segment has low EVA and growth, but it is less likely that a company can be successful with its strategies to outperform its competitors.

Mass consumption, retail

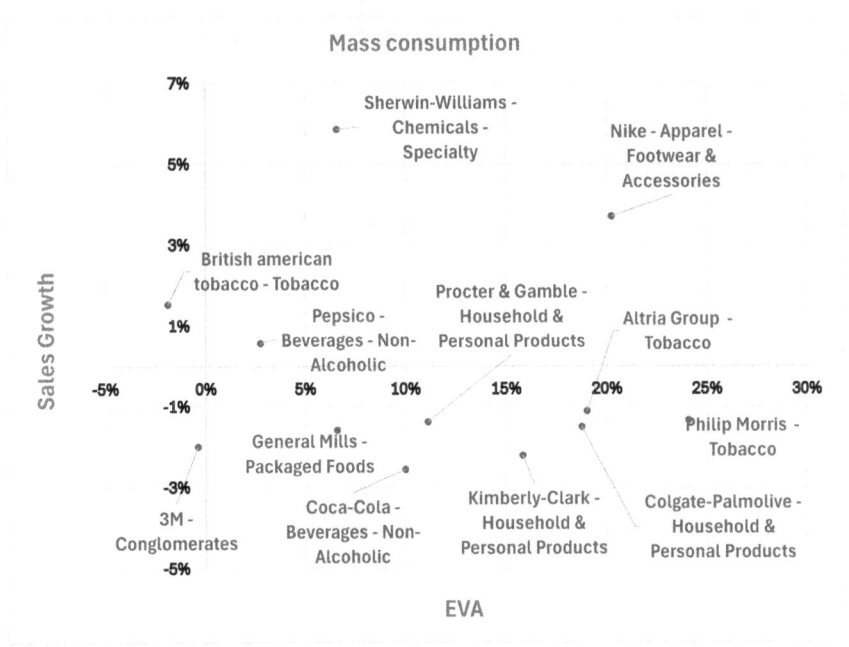

Mass consumption

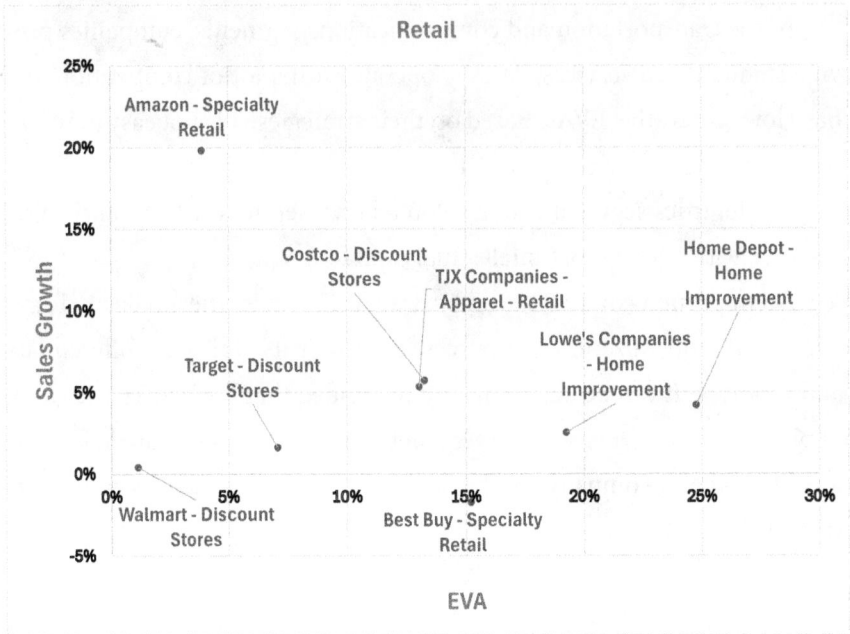

**Figure 12. Economic value creation,
mass consumption segments, retail trade.**

These two segments have much more intellectual capital and, therefore, greater capacity for innovation and differentiation, so it is possible to find companies like Amazon with higher growth rates.

Health, leisure.

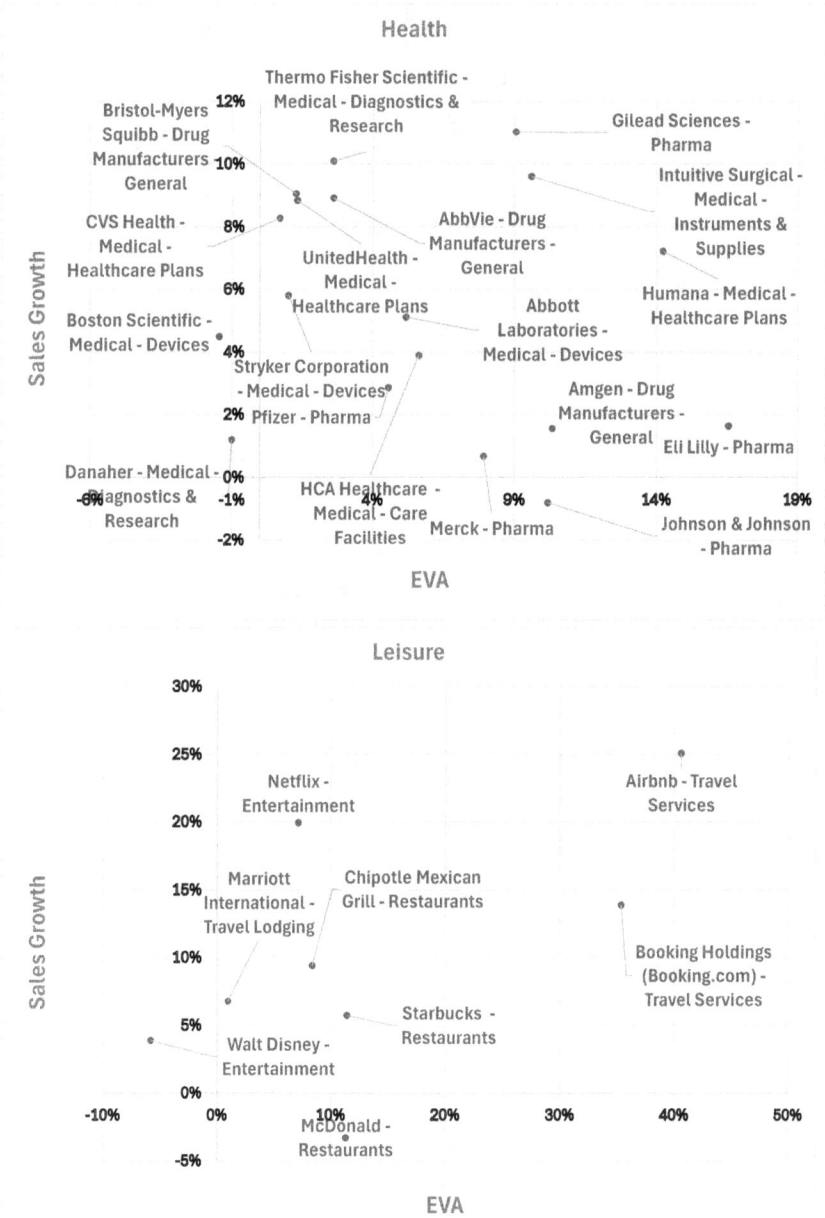

Figure 13. Economic value creation, health, and leisure segments

These two segments have greater intellectual capital, greater capacity to develop knowledge and relationships, and thus greater capacity for innovation and differentiation, which leads some companies to be successful with their strategies.

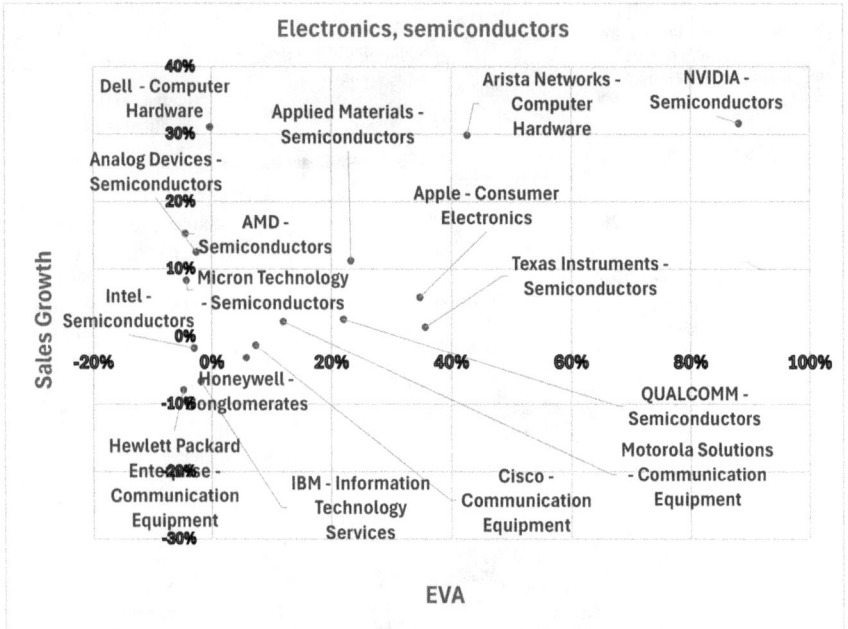

Figure 14. Economic value creation, electronics, and semiconductor segments.

Electronics, semiconductors

In this segment, there is a struggle between intellectual and physical capital, the innovation of companies such as Nvidia, which has a very high EVA and growth rate, and the standardization of many other companies that sell commodities, such as Dell or Hewlett-Packard.

Software

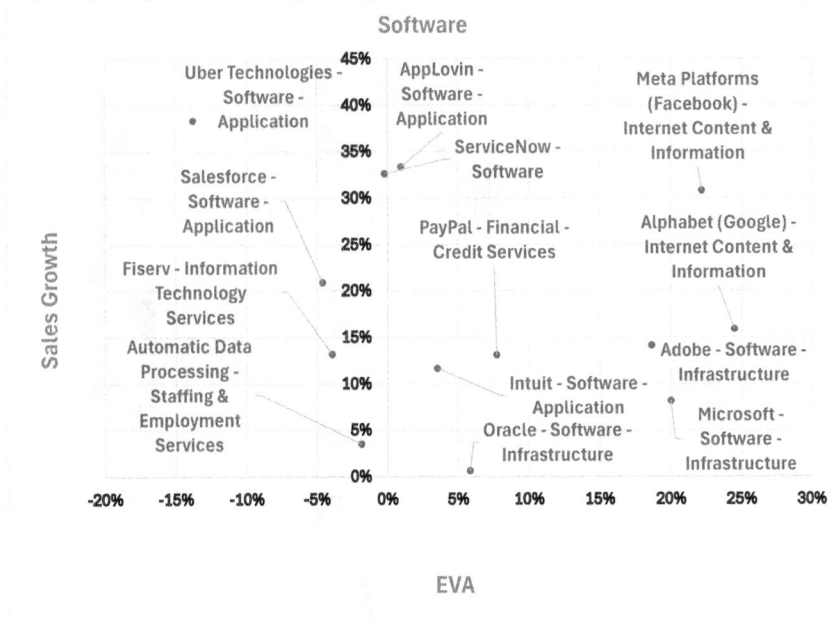

Figure 15. Economic value creation, software segment.

Software is pure intellectual capital, with a much higher capacity for innovation and differentiation, as demonstrated by cases such as Meta, Alphabet (Google), Adobe, and Microsoft. Therefore, EVAs and growth can be very high.

Next steps in experiential learning

The reader can continue the exercise following the methodology in Appendix 1.

Once EVA and sales growth have been calculated, the reader can analyze the possible strategies for each company and frame them in Figure 16, relying on information from specialized websites (Morningstar, Yahoo Finance, Seeking Alpha, Zacks Investment Research, TradingView, Finviz,

GuruFocus, Simply Wall St.) or artificial intelligence such as ChatGPT or Perplexity.

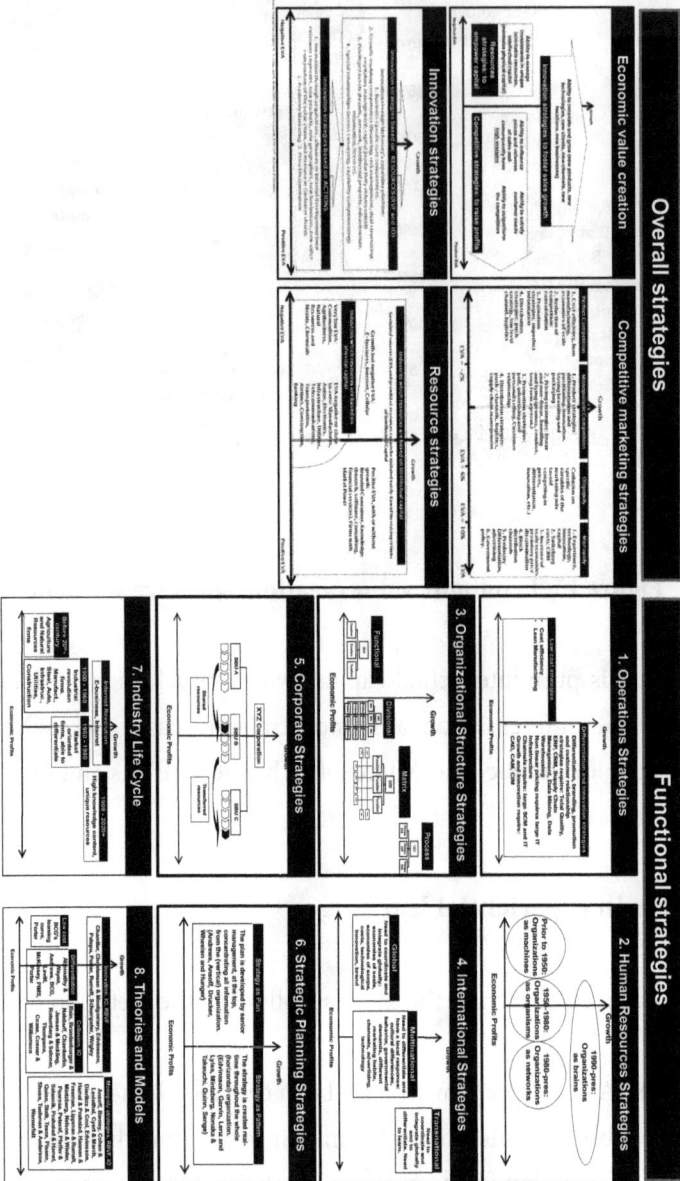

Figure 16. Environments, strategies and economic value creation. General and functional strategies.

Conclusions

This exercise is very important:

1. We have succeeded in establishing a bridge between economic value creation and strategic management, which incorporates metrics, rationality, and critical and interdisciplinary thinking, key competencies of all managers. From now on, we only need to link the three core strategies, competitive, innovation, and resources, with three metrics: EVA, Sales Growth, and MVA (Market Value Added = Intellectual Capital).

2. We have managed to simplify and unite strategic management with functional strategies: strategic environments, strategies, and their results are summarized on one page.

3. This is extremely valuable; moreover, if one wants to invest in shares of these companies, if one plans to develop a new business, or if one has the possibility of working in one of these companies or business segments.

This exercise helps to raise awareness of the importance of economic value creation. If we had calculated the EVAs of all existing companies in the USA instead of this small sample of the 120 most successful companies, the average EVA of the entire universe would give us an EVA of 0%. This is very shocking: half of all companies destroy economic value, including modern, cutting-edge companies, which creates many difficulties for them, as we will see below.

Consequently, we can expect that around 50% of organizations destroy economic value because they are unable to position themselves above average. However, a precise figure is impossible to provide, as it depends on each market.

Chapter 4

Experiential Learning. Analyzing the Dynamics of Value Creation, the Past and the Future.

In this third experiential learning, we are introduced to the dynamic part, the past, and the future. This is key to strategic decision making, where the connection between strategies and future results makes the most sense. Strategic management has been repeatedly criticized for serving to analyze the past but not helping to visualize the future.

The website jps.net has a financial simulation developed by Juan Carlos Torviso (Master of Finance, Stanford University). This simulation is part of my previous book, *Strategic Value Management. Economic value Creation and the Management of the Firm.* [1]

This simulation projects an organization's financial statements for the next 20 years and produces the economic value creation graphs we have seen above, allowing us to analyze and understand the economic value creation process in depth.

For purely academic purposes, I have simulated the value creation of Starbucks[2] in an optimistic and pessimistic environment. Both simulations are at https://www.juanpablostegmann.net/

---

[1] Stegmann, Juan. P. *Strategic Value Management. Economic Value Creation and the Management of the Firm.* Hoboken, N. J. John Wiley and Sons. 2009.

Juan Carlos Torviso developed the simulation presented in the book.

[2] The following link provides a video explaining how this financial simulation works: https://www.juanpablostegmann.net/documents?lightbox=dataItem-k9kboses4

The first year of the simulation reflects Starbucks' historical financial statements. I have simulated the following years, which are based on my opinion and are not intended to describe Starbucks' reality. I have tried to make the market value indicated by the simulation similar to the actual market value of the company so that the simulation can reflect how an investor might view the future of the company.

Optimistic scenario. How economic value is created.

The following graphs are produced by the simulation. They help to visualize what could happen in an optimistic scenario.

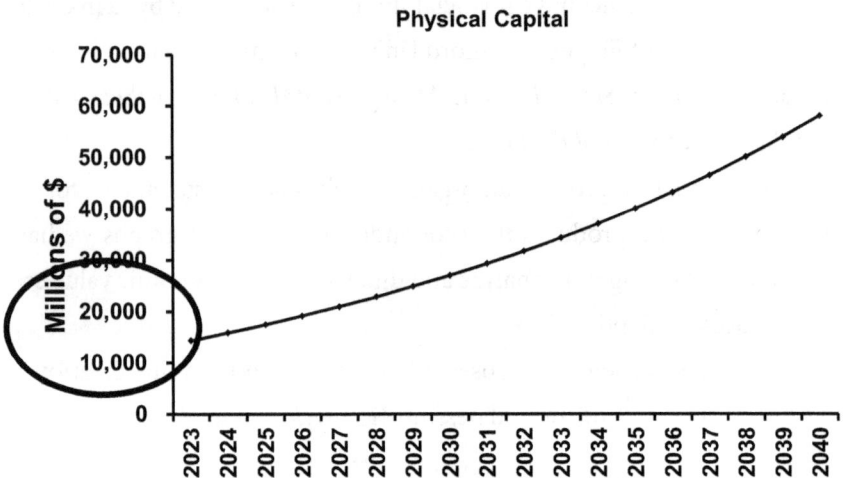

Figure 17. Starbucks' physical capital evolution years 2022 to 2040.

Figure 17 shows that Starbucks must invest $15 billion in physical capital in the first year and higher values in subsequent years.

Here is the simulation with the Starbucks data I have incorporated: https://www.juanpablostegmann.net/documents?lightbox=dataItem-k9kbew3m1

In this last link, a video is available to understand the EVA model.

However, we do not know whether this decision is good or bad, as we do not know whether Starbucks can create economic value.

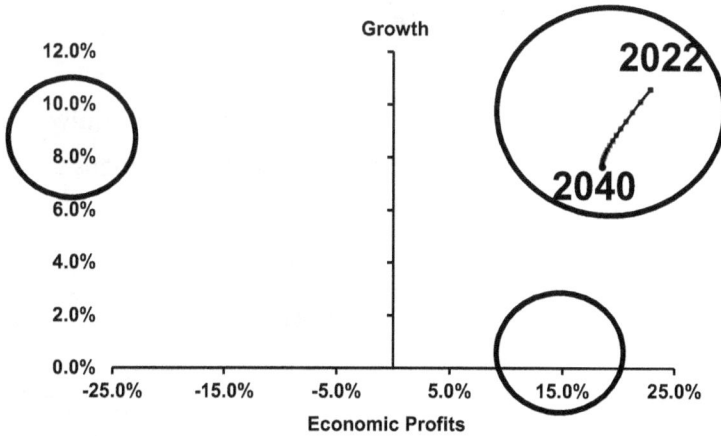

Figure 18. Starbucks' economic value creation years 2022 to 2040.

Figure 18 shows Starbucks' ability to create economic value: economic profits (EVA) will be around 20% in the next few years, which is outstanding; the other component is growth, which will be around 10% in the next few years, which is also excellent.

According to this simulation, investors consider Starbucks to have strong economic value creation capabilities.

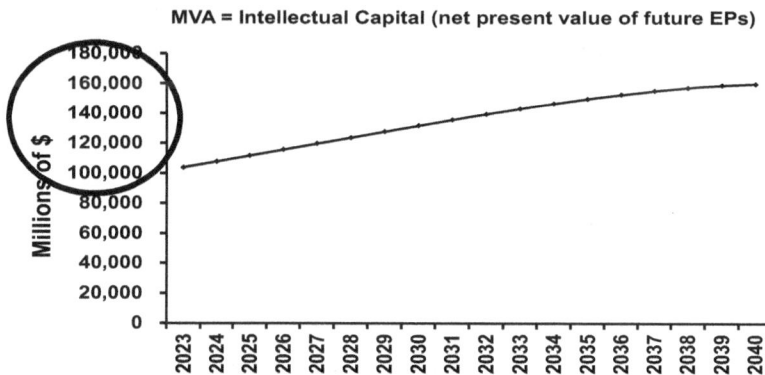

**Figure 19. Evolution of intellectual capital (MVA)
of Starbucks years 2022 to 2040.**

Figure 19 reflects Starbucks' Market Value Added (MVA), its intellectual capital. The MVA is calculated as the market value of the organization over its book value, or as the EVA model puts it, the net present value of future economic benefits.

This excellent intellectual capital reflects investors' positive view of Starbucks' prospects. Intellectual capital (knowledge, relationships, innovation and processes) is the backbone of its competitive and innovation strategies.

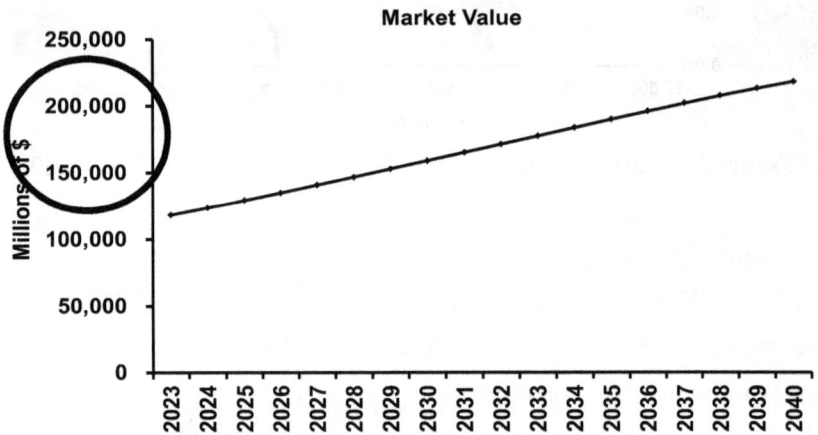

Figure 20. Evolution of Starbucks market value years 2022 to 2040.

Figure 20 shows that Starbucks' market value = physical capital + intellectual capital, will increase from $120 billion in the first year to $220 billion in the last year, which is also a valid indicator of the success of its strategies.

Pessimistic scenario. How economic value is destroyed.

The Figures below help to visualize what would happen in a pessimistic scenario.

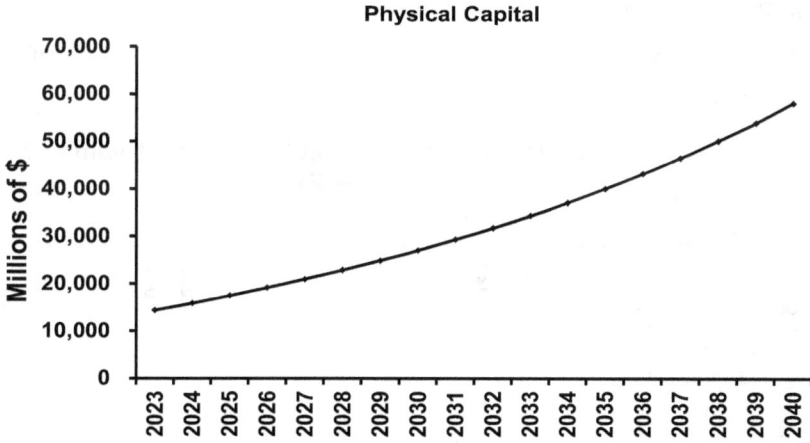

Figure 21. Starbucks' physical capital evolution years 2022 to 2040.

Figure 21 shows that Starbucks must invest $15 billion in physical capital during the first year and higher values during the following years.

However, we do not know whether this decision is good or bad, as we do not know whether Starbucks can create economic value.

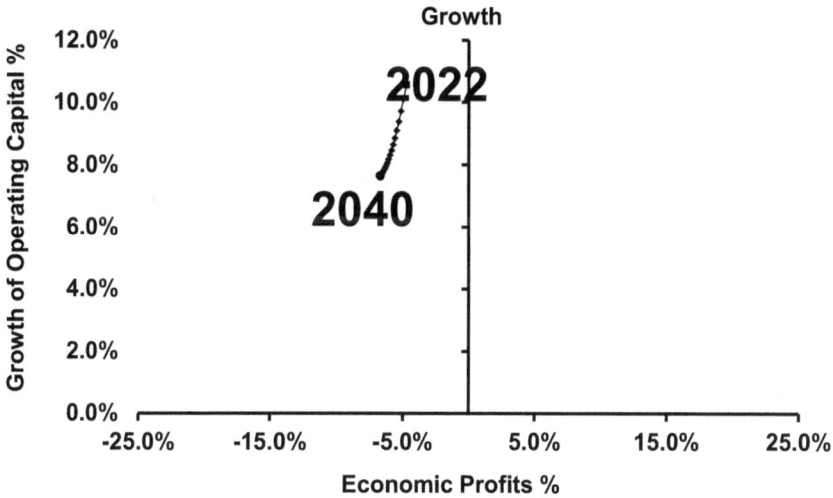

Figure 22. Starbucks' economic value creation years 2022 to 2040.

Figure 22 shows that the economic benefits (EVA) for the next few years will be negative, between -4% and -6%; growth will be around 10% for the next few years.

MVA = Intellectual Capital (net present value of future EVAs)

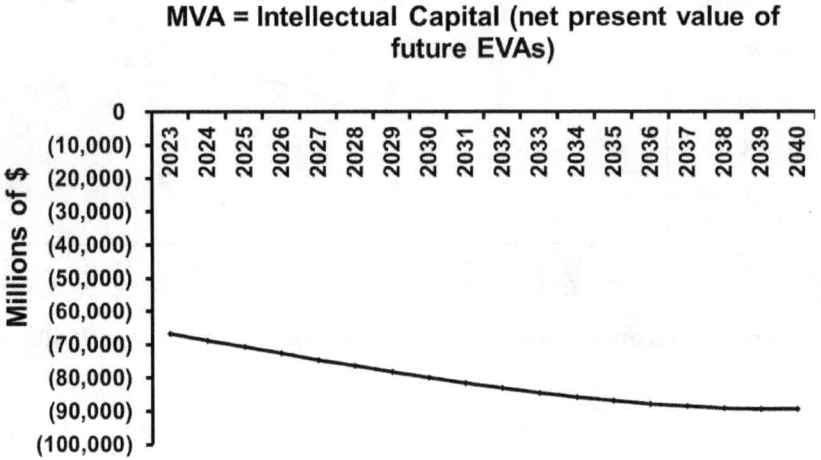

Figure 23. Evolution of Starbucks' intellectual capital (MVA) years 2022 to 2040.

Figure 23 shows a strongly negative intellectual capital (MVA). It indicates that Starbucks lacks unique resources to sustain competitive and innovation strategies.

Market Value

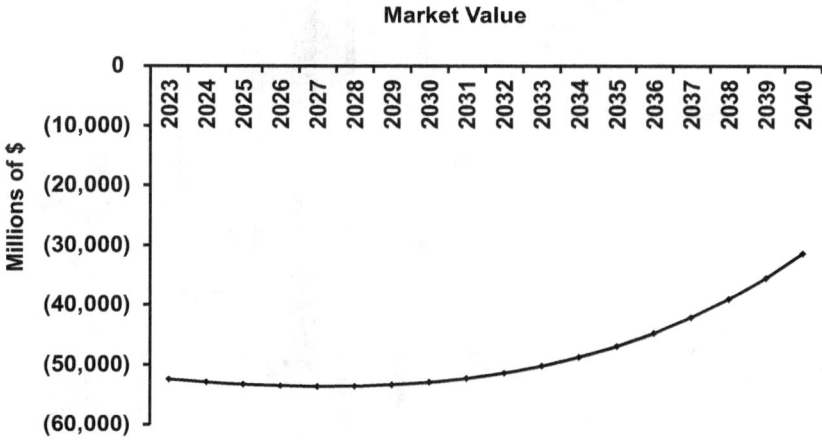

Figure 24. Evolution of Starbucks' market value years 2022 to 2040.

Figure 24 shows that Starbucks' market value will be negative, the latest indication of its failed strategies.

Analyzing the future

The second experiential exercise we did, summarizing the strategies on one page, is enhanced when we use the financial simulation and then extrapolate the results to analyze future strategies. Figure 25 shows the recommended strategies in the optimistic and pessimistic examples we discussed above, for the next 20 years.

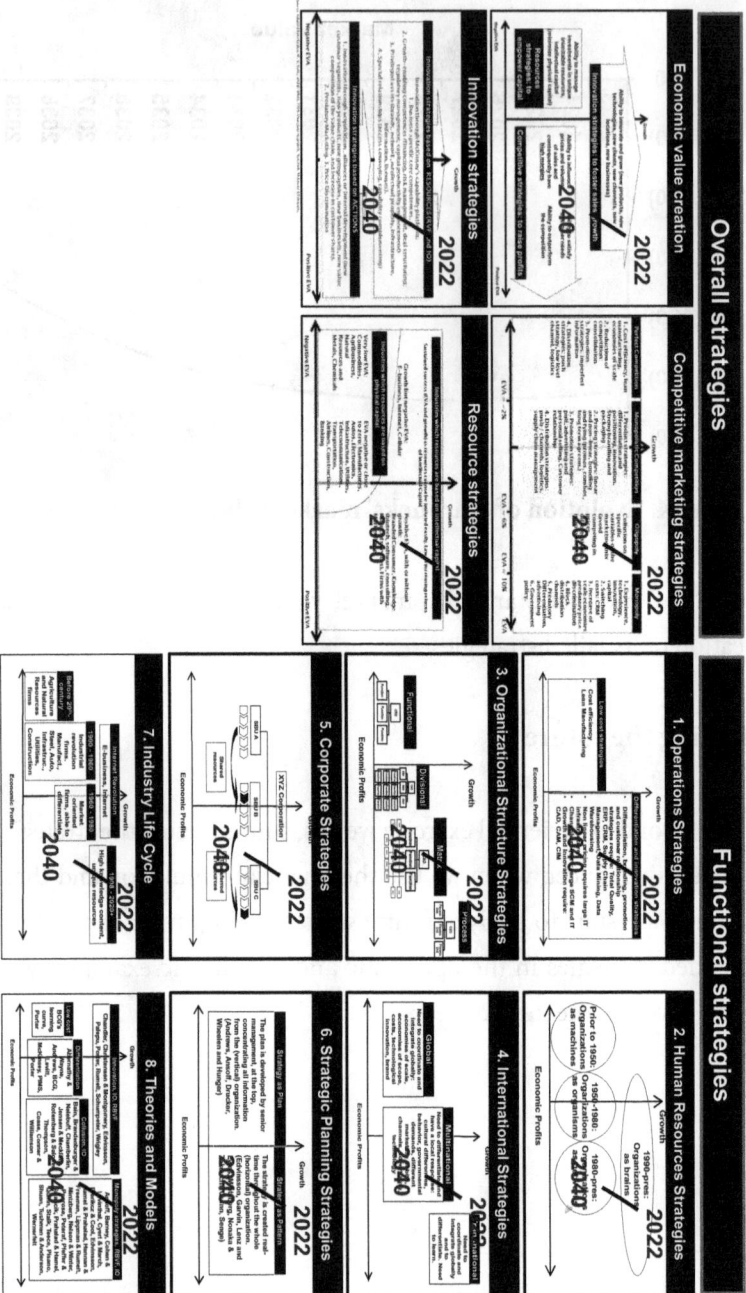

Figure 25. Evolution of Starbucks market value years 2022 to 2040.

Analyzing the past

This also helps us to analyze the past and to link past economic results with their strategies.

The reader can visualize Figure 26, the value creation of some well-known companies, and analyze the past, using information from specialized websites or AI, as discussed in the first experiential exercise: several dot.coms such as Amazon, Nvidia, Netflix, Google had enormous growth during the pandemic; Microsoft and Coca Cola have had high market power (high EVAs), but with little growth, etc.

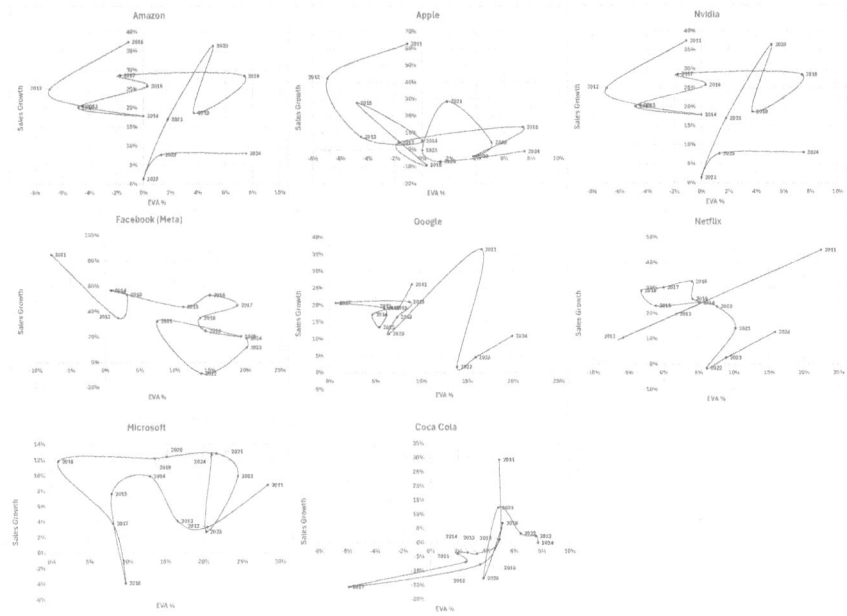

Figure 26. Evolution of some leading companies
past economic value creation.

Conclusions

The reader can use this simulation to analyze the future of other companies or new ventures, and determine whether their future strategies can create economic value.

This allows the analysis of past and future environments, strategies, and results of segments and companies.

It even allows the analysis of strategies that are not contemplated in these charts: for example, if a company expects to have negative EVAs in the future, it can analyze its future financial strategies, such as financing itself with self-generated funds instead of issuing shares, and even eventually delisting the company from the stock market.

Conclusions. 1. Building critical and interdisciplinary thinking, a key competency of all managers.

We have discussed a new version of Capstone, which introduces a framework for developing critical and interdisciplinary thinking.

Critical thinking

Critical thinking is a key competency of every manager. Modern culture, universities, the world of organizations, and strategic management promote critical thinking in decision-making.

The Encyclopedia Britannica links critical thinking to the exercise of dissent; the Stanford Encyclopedia of Philosophy links it to the "Critical Thinking Movement," which seeks to inform and enhance public reasoning and debate by promoting models of education that emphasize critical examination of beliefs and decisions, and the development of the skills this requires. Critical thinking is an intellectual activity. We receive information, we analyze it with a critical attitude.

The critical thinking posed by this version of strategic management arises from the following factors:

- The incorporation of metrics is a source of critical thinking, by putting a numerical value on environments, strategies and results, which leads to questioning the proposed strategies. This makes it possible to overcome the qualitative, ambiguous and conceptual approach of traditional strategic management.
- By incorporating real-world metrics, linked to the value of companies listed on stock markets, or metrics that arise from accounting, it resolves a problem that strategic management has been

questioned for years: its disconnection from reality and inability to predict an organization's future.

- Relying on Industrial Economics models and metrics provides critical thinking. For example, Stephen Martin presents the following model to describe innovation, linking environment, strategies and outcomes, promoting critical thinking; according to the model, innovation only works if the innovating firm has market power: $E = (n - 1) V [r + (n - 2) h]/(r + nh)3 + \{2V [(r + (n - 1) h]/(r + nh)3 + dF2 /dh2 \} > 0$

- Systems thinking is a source of critical thinking, as it leads to questioning the coherence between environments, general strategies (competitive, innovation, resource strategies), functional strategies (marketing, operations, human resources, organizations, strategic planning) and results (economic value creation).

- The "economic benefits" metric used in the EVA model is a source of critical thinking because it forces a comparison of the organization's results with similar organizations. Economic benefits involve the "opportunity cost," which compares the benefits of using resources in an organization or strategy versus other alternatives.

- Showing that theories, models, and strategies are contingent on the environment, strategies, and outcomes is a powerful source of critical thinking.

Interdisciplinary thinking

Allen Repko, an expert in interdisciplinary research, and Erving Goffman, an expert in qualitative analysis, recommend the use of these models to foster interdisciplinary thinking. As this Part 1 showed, the incorporation of a conceptual model allows, for example, a marketing specialist to relate his or her marketing strategy to all other business strategies.

Interdisciplinarity generates critical thinking, as it allows other disciplines such as political economy, finance, ethics or social responsibility to question the validity of strategies.

Discernment

This exercise in critical thinking and interdisciplinary thinking opens the way to incorporate discernment in decision making.

What is discernment? According to the most popular dictionaries:

- Collins. It is the ability to judge which things of a certain type are good and which are bad.
- Webster. The power or faculty of the mind, by which it distinguishes one thing from another, as truth from falsehood, virtue from vice; acuteness of judgment; power of perceiving differences of things or ideas, and their relations and tendencies.
- Encyclopedia Britannica. The ability to see and understand people, things or situations clearly and intelligently.
- Cambridge. It is the ability to judge people and things well.
- Merrian - Webster. It is the quality of being able to understand what is obscure.

ChatGPT and Perplexity summarize the components of discernment, such as: taking your time, clarity of thought, weighing motives, awareness of values, prayer/reflection, community/dialogue, self-awareness, attention to desires, openness/freedom, discernment of spirits.

The continuation of this book, "A new capstone - Decision making with discernment" presents a broader and deeper vision of what discernment is:

1. The cognitive dimension of our discernment. Incorporating knowledge, awareness, and wisdom in our decisions.

2. The transcendental dimension of our discernment. Incorporating ideals in our decisions, the journey to goodness, beauty, and truth.

3. The axiological dimension of our discernment. Incorporating our values and culture into our decisions.

4. The religious dimension of our discernment. Living in the presence of God, and building our relationship with him.

5. The relational dimension. Incorporating consciousness and community in our decisions.

6. The decisional dimension of our discernment. Incorporating our interiority in our decisions.

7. The existential dimension of our discernment. Incorporating the meaning of life in our decisions.

8. The transformative dimension of our discernment. Incorporating our power to create, recreate, transform in our decisions.

9. The healing dimension of our discernment. Incorporating our healing capacity of spirit, mind, and body in our decisions.

10. The social action dimension of our discernment. Incorporating our capacity to execute social actions into our decisions.

In other words, discernment leads us to humanize our decision-making.

Conclusions. 2. Resources help predict the future of an organization.

Resource strategies are a key dimension of critical thinking in strategic management, enabling the prediction of an organization's future success or failure.

Often, a paradox can be observed: when evaluating the current results of an organization, all indicators appear favorable. However, the value of the company's shares has performed poorly. There seems to be no explanation until one examines the resources: they serve as a crystal ball, helping to predict the future.

Resources are the backbone of competitive and growth strategies. How can they help predict the future? What role can resources play in supporting competitive and growth strategies?

SWOT strengths arise from the unique resources a company has that make it stronger than its competitors. These unique resources provide a company with greater benefits than its competitors.

SWOT opportunities arise from a company's ability to leverage factors or players in the external environment, including economic, political, regulatory, demand, technological, and other factors. For example, in a recession, a company that supplies systems that help reduce costs can be very successful: the internal resources of that company allow it to transform an external factor such as the recession into a business opportunity. Another example is that the pandemic helped Amazon grow.

In short, companies with the right resources can grow based on their resources, transforming external environmental factors into business opportunities.

Conclusions. 3. Importance of this new version of strategic management for future decision making.

This new version of strategic management is revolutionary.

- Simplifies all strategic management by presenting all strategies on a single page.
- It allows checking the compatibility of all strategies.
- It allows us to analyze which strategies we can use to create economic value.
- It promotes crucial competencies for managers: critical and strategic thinking, and facilitates discernment, a crucial competency that all leaders should have.
- It promotes a crucial competence for managers: interdisciplinary thinking that links several disciplines: finance, marketing, operations, political economy, leadership, spirituality, philosophy, and psychology. This allows for linking strategies with each other and with the models and theories of the science of strategic management, providing intellectual support, and adopting a contingent approach: which theories apply to the strategies I am proposing, thereby eliminating a common mistake of thinking that all strategies must be used, which is a passport to failure.
- Incorporating resources links strategic management with political economy, which we will discuss in Part 2, where the success of organizations requires resources in terms of intellectual capital.
- By incorporating resources and processes, strategic management can be linked to leadership, also based on processes, as we will see in Part 3.
- Critical thinking and intellectual capital prepare us for the book "A new Capstone - Decision making with discernment", which

teaches us how to move from critical thinking to discernment, which is crucial for decision making.

- This provides the following benefits:
- Clarity of ideas. Connecting the environment and strategies with results in terms of economic value creation is conceptually crucial. Professionals have a powerful analytical tool to make strategic decisions, knowing what results are expected.
- Simplicity. Simplifies and integrates strategic management, solving the lack of unity of traditional strategic management, the atomization of theories and models, and the disconnection with functional strategies. It consolidates and unifies all strategies, grouping them into three categories: competitive strategies, responsible for profitability; innovation strategies, responsible for sales growth; and resource strategies, responsible for capital allocation. This approach helps resolve the atomization of the current literature on the subject and explains the differences between theories as part of a contingent approach. All strategic management models can be framed within the EVA metric, providing an integrated and coherent view of an organization's entire management.
- Knowledge integration. Resolves the lack of interdisciplinary thinking in traditional strategic management and functional strategies. By incorporating the central role of resources, specifically intellectual capital and its components—human capital, social capital, renewal capital, and process capital—it promotes interdisciplinary thinking, as resources impact multiple disciplines.
- Rationality. Provides metrics and cause-effect connections, linking the strategic environment, strategies, and results. Demonstrates that different strategic management models, theories, and strategies produce different results in terms of economic value creation.

- Practicality. The criticism that strategic management seems to be a soft discipline is now replaced by a practical vision of strategic management with concrete metrics.
- The social dimension of strategic management. It allows introducing the social impact of strategic management, providing the connection between strategies and results, and connecting strategic management with social disciplines such as ethics and corporate social responsibility.
- Relevance for non-business organizations. This new version of strategic management is also valid for non-business, non-profit organizations, individuals, communities, governments, NGOs, armed forces, clubs, churches and other agents.

Part 2

An Integrating Political Economy that Maximizes Social Well-Being

Introduction

Part 2 incorporates the political economy into the Capstone, becoming a crucial piece of the decision-making.

Part 1 demonstrated the centrality of intellectual capital to the success of organizations and provides financial justification for measuring it in terms of MVA; Part 2 provides important research support to explain the first two dimensions of intellectual capital: human capital and social capital.

Intellectual capital is the backbone of a nation's success, its economic growth, and social justice. With this, political economy ends a decades-long debate between the left and the right and focuses on how to create intellectual capital. Both left and right have strengths and weaknesses: nations must build intellectual capital to reduce their weaknesses and reinforce their strengths.

This Part 2 summarizes the thinking of several leading economists and Nobel laureates[1].

It expands on the Capstone by drawing on leading authors' thinking to understand why intellectual capital is crucial to the success of nations and organizations.

---

[1] Ronald Coase (1991), Gary Becker (1992), Douglass North (1993), Amartya Sen (1998), Thomas Schelling and Robert Aumann (2005), Oliver E. Williamson (2009), and Paul Romer (2018), Daron Acemoglu, Simon Johnson, and James Robinson (2024).

71

This prepares Module 2 of this book, "Decision making with discernment", which analyzes how discernment promotes the creation of intellectual capital of organizations and nations.

Chapter 1

Experiential learning

The business model proposed by Leif Edvinsson, which we discussed in Part 1, summarizes an organization's strategic plan and balanced scorecard. As summarized in Figure 26, the business model shows that an organization's success is reflected in its ability to create intellectual capital.

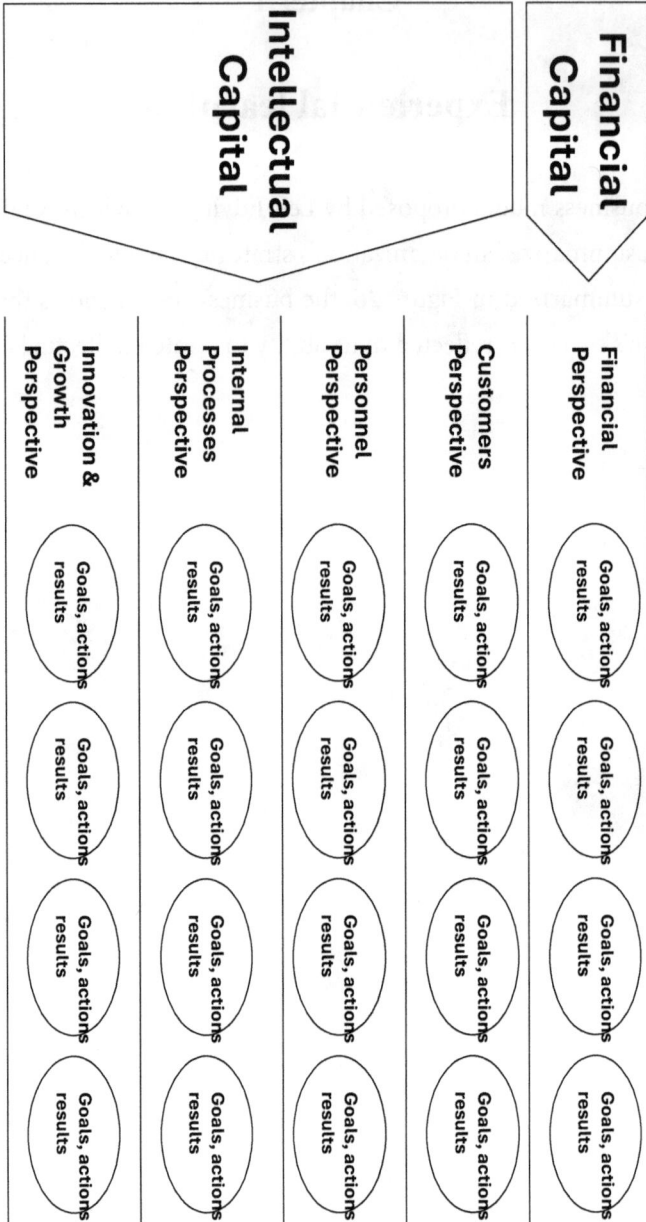

Figure 26. Business model and economic value creation.

Table 2 presents a similar intuition but applied to nations.

	Human Capital	Market Capital	Process Capital	Renewal Capital	Financial Capital	Total
Sweden	8.38	6.38	7.26	7.97	9.66	39.65
Finland	7.76	6.52	7.73	7.79	9.59	39.38
Switzerland	7.58	6.39	7.38	8	9.76	39.1
Denmark	8.61	6.6	7.61	6.2	9.68	38.69
Singapore	7.01	8.34	7.51	5.13	9.9	37.9
USA	7.84	5.65	6.85	7.11	9.9	37.34
Iceland	8.09	6.56	7.03	5.91	9.7	37.31
Israel	7.82	5.72	6.39	7.06	9.4	36.39
Netherlands	7.27	6.8	7	5.19	9.74	36.02
Canada	8.06	6.24	4.6	5	9.72	35.62
Norway	7.96	5.87	6.93	4.76	10	35.52
Austria	7.11	6.31	6.99	5.01	9.71	35.14
Australia	7.34	6.22	11	4.63	9.69	34.95
Ireland	6.96	7.05	6.89	3.93	9.78	34.65
Japan	7.34	4.78	5.94	6.52	9.58	34.18
Germany	6.52	5.51	6.37	5.75	9.62	33.8
Taiwan	6.87	5.9	6.28	5.04	9.45	33.59
Belgium	7.34	5.66	6	4.78	9.64	33.45
UNITED KINGDOM	6.59	5.39	6.24	4.53	9.63	32.44
New Zealand	6.93	5.98	6.23	3.63	9.38	32.2
France	6.79	4.4	5.73	4.67	9.6	31.21
Korea	6.75	5.07	5.35	4.2	9.31	30.71
Spain	6.30	5.05	5.37	2.6	9.49	28.83
Malaysia	6.03	6.48	5.34	2.07	8.69	28.69

Czech Republic	5.7	5.61	5.26	2.68	9.2	28.49
Hungary	6.56	5.37	5.12	2.37	9.01	28.44
Italy	6.23	4.44	5.34	2.62	9.53	28.18
Portugal	6.36	4.89	5.36	2.08	9.25	27.97
Chile	5.23	6.63	5.16	1.72	8.74	27.49
Greece	5.78	4.48	4.56	2.11	9.4	26.37
Thailand	5.11	5.7	4.31	1.39	8.18	24.71
South Africa	4.85	4.96	4.33	1.73	8.41	24.28
Poland	5.92	3.94	3.52	1.85	8.85	24.17
Russia	5.46	4.06	3.21	2.59	8.69	24.01
Turkey	4.53	4.93	3.86	1.54	8.6	23.48
China	4.35	5.22	3.72	2.03	7.71	23.1
Mexico	4.87	4.72	3.18	1.21	8.76	22.79
Brazil	4.52	4.64	3.11	1.72	8.44	22.45
India	3.93	5.25	3.38	1.88	7.12	21.56
Philippines	4.94	4.58	3.2	1.34	7.41	21.45
Argentina	5.11	3.35	2.7	1.43	8.64	21.24

Table 2. National Intellectual Capital of 41 countries

Source Edvinsson, Leif; Yeh-Yun Lin, Carol. "Modeling and Measurement of National Intellectual Capital" in International Journal of Knowledge-Based Development 3, 1 (2012): 72-73.

National intellectual capital as an integral vision of resources

Leif Edvinsson defines national intellectual capital as the engine of a nation's economic growth:

- National Intellectual Capital (future welfare potential):
  - Human Capital (people's capacity and skills)
  - Structural Capital:
    - Market capital (global business attractiveness)
    - Organization's capital:
      - Renewal Capital (creation, exploitation and innovation of knowledge)
      - Process Capital (operational functionality of the company)

National intellectual capital consists mainly of five types of capital: human capital, market capital, process capital, renewal capital and financial capital.

- **Human capital** includes the knowledge, wisdom, experience, intuition, and capacity of individuals to accomplish national tasks and goals. It also includes the values embodied in a nation's culture and philosophy. Human capital constitutes the total capabilities of a population reflected in education, knowledge, health, experience, motivation, intuition, entrepreneurship, and expertise. It is captured through indicators such as a highly-skilled labor force, availability of scientists and engineers, female labor force participation, and health (life expectancy, doctors). Human capital provides the resources for the development and cultivation of other areas of intellectual assets, such as R&D and training, with the human factor being the most critical link in the value creation process.
- **Structural capital** is the value of what is left in an organization when the employees - the human capital - have gone home. It

includes databases, customer lists, manuals, brands, and organizational structures.

- **Market capital** refers to the overall assets embodied in a nation's relationship with the international market. It is the sum of a country's capabilities and successes in offering an attractive and competitive solution to the needs of its international customers, a country's investments and achievements in foreign relations, and its exports of quality products and services (Bontis 2004). Intangible assets here include customer or country loyalty, openness to globalization, flexibility and adaptability, the resilience of the economy, as well as satisfaction expressed by strategic customers and domestic business partners.

- **Organizational capital** refers to systematized and packaged competence and systems to leverage the company's innovative strength and organizational capacity for value creation. It consists of process capital, culture, and innovation capital.

- **Renewal capital** refers to a nation's capabilities and investments to increase its competitive strength in future markets, fostering future growth. Renewal and development assets include R&D investments, patents, trademarks, start-ups, scientific publications, U.S. patents filed, EPO patent applications, total R&D spending, and innovation capacity.

- **Process capital** is the cooperation and flow of knowledge that requires structural intellectual assets. These include information systems, hardware, software, databases, laboratories, national infrastructure including transportation, information technology skills, communications and computerization, technology readiness and telecommunications services, personal computers, cell phone subscribers, cyber security, quality scientific research institutions, knowledge transfer, a legal environment for entrepreneurship, a minimum number of days to start a business, a quality management system, and agricultural productivity. These structural intellectual assets sustain and enhance the performance of human capital."[1]

According to Eskil Ullberg, Leif Edvinsson and Carol Yeh-Yun Linmore, more than 70% of the value created in Sweden comes from NIC, which is 60% higher than physical assets and more than 200% higher than financial assets . According to them, the secret recipe for Nordic success lies mainly in intangibles.[2]

---

[1] Ullberg, Eskil; Edvinsson, Leif; Yeh-Yun Lin, Carol. *Intangible Asset Gap in Global Competitiveness. Mapping and Responding to the New Economy.* Springer Briefs in Business. 2021.

[2] Ibid. pp. 15-17.

Chapter 2

Economic Growth is based on resources.

Several theories explain how economic growth is based on resources. Modern political economy proposes two fundamental resources to foster economic growth: human capital and social capital.

Robert Solow (Massachusetts Institute of Technology) published a seminal research paper on economic growth and development: "A Contribution to the Theory of Economic Growth". This paper explores how economic growth is based on factors external to the system: technology, human capital, financial capital and means of production.

Gregory Mankiw, David Romer and David Weil, in a later paper ("A Contribution to the Empirics of Economic Growth"), show that the model must include human capital and skilled labor as critical resources. For Jones and Vollrath[1] human capital, expressed in the qualification of labor, plays an essential role in explaining worker productivity and influencing economic growth.

---

[1] The following equation presented by Charles Jones and Dietrich Vollrath summarizes that approach:

$y^*(t) = (sK / n + g + d)^{(a) (/ 1-a)}hA(t)$

$y^*(t)$: production/technology ratio per worker

sK:the rate of investment in physical capital

g: technological progress index

h: job skills

Jones, Charles I.; Vollrath, Dietrich. *Economic Growth*. New York, London. W. W. Norton & Company. 2013. p. 57.

According to Paul Romer,[2] it is knowledge that increases technology and human skills. For Jones and Vollrath,[3] economic growth requires capital, skilled labor and knowledge/ideas. This makes technology an endogenous factor: technology is the result of research and new ideas created by individuals to foster economic prosperity.

Knowledge has several benefits. First, it can generate increasing returns because each new unit of production does not require relevant costs, or its costs may be zero. For example, once a piece of music or a computer program has been created, it can be stored on a CD at low cost and sold at a high price, generating increasing returns.

Secondly, knowledge can produce positive externalities, since other organizations can benefit from its creation without investing in it. For example, once *smartphones* are created, several companies can sell applications specially designed for them.

---

[2] Romer, Paul M. "Increasing Returns and Long-Run Growth" in *Journal of Political Economy* 94 (1986): 1002-37.

"Endogenous Technological Change" in *Journal of Political Economy* 98 (1990): S71-S102.

"The Origins of Endogenous Growth" in *Journal of Economic Perspectives* 8 (1994): 3-22.

[3] The following equation presented by Charles Jones and Dietrich Vollrath summarizes that approach:

$Y = {}^{(Ka)}(A\ L)^{1-a}$

Y: production

K: capital

L: work

A: knowledge, ideas

Jones, Charles I.; Vollrath, Dietrich. *Economic Growth*. New York, London. W. W. Norton & Company. 2013. p. 99.

Third, knowledge can increase with the growth of an educated population: the more educated people there are in a country, the greater the chances of having a more significant knowledge production.

All these factors have a positive impact on a country's economic growth.

Human capital promotes economic growth

Human capital is the first critical resource needed to promote economic growth. The concept of human capital was introduced by Adam Smith, who considered talents and education as part of the capital of the individual and of society.

Robert Solow[4] shows that, during the 20TH century, much of the growth cannot be explained by physical capital; later research shows that human capital is responsible.

Gregory Mankiw, David Romer, and David Weil[5] extended Solow's model by introducing human capital, which yields better results in terms of income growth and productivity.

Robert Lucas Jr. and Paul Romer add skills and knowledge as part of human capital, which impact productivity and technological progress, and increase rates of return.

Gary Becker explains that human capital refers to the knowledge, information, ideas, skills, and health of individuals, which raises productivity and income growth.[6]

---

[4] Solow, Robert. "Technical Change and the Aggregate Production Function" in *The Review of Economics and Statistics* 39, 3 (1957): 312-320.

[5] Mankiw, N. Gregory; Romer, David; Weil, David N. "A Contribution To The Empirics Of Economic Growth" in *The Quarterly Journal of Economics,* 107, 2 (1992): 407-437, https://doi.org/10.2307/2118477

[6] Ibid. p. 24.

Theodore Schultz argues for the importance of human capital, including health, schooling, adult education, on-the-job training, and migration, in promoting economic growth.

Mincer developed the "schooling model," which posits that human capital, based on education and training, has a positive impact on the economy.

Eric A. Hanushek and Ludger Woessmann[7] studied the impact of schooling and cognitive skills on economic growth. They conclude that: "Cognitive skills have powerful effects on people's income, income distribution and economic growth".

According to Clifford and Novaro, "Human capital is the set of skills, knowledge, and social and personality attributes, including creativity, that is embodied in the ability to perform work to produce economic value."[8]

Social capital promotes economic growth (endogenous growth)

Mancur Olson introduced the role of institutions as a fundamental factor in the economic success of countries: "The most important explanation for the differences in income between countries is the difference in their economic policies and institutions. [9]

---

[7] Hanushek, Eric A. and Ludger Woessmann. "The Role of Cognitive Skills in Economic Development" in *Journal of Economic Literature* 46, 3 (2008): 607-668.

[8] Clifford, Nyone B. and Rosemaria C. Obaro. "Human Capital Development on Employee Performance," in *Proceedings of the Second American Academic Research Conference on Global Business, Economics, Finance and Social Sciences* (AAR17 New York Conference), (2017): 28-30, efaidnbmnnnibpcajpcglclefindmkaj/https://globalbizresearch.org/New_York_Conferences_2017_April1/docs/doc/3.%20Management/N752.pdf.

[9] Ibid. p. 7.

Robert Barro[10] made an outstanding contribution in his famous paper "Determinants of Economic Growth". According to Barro, growth is positively associated with property rights, civic and political freedom, which are parameters of levels of democracy.

Nieswiadomy and Strazicich[11] also analyze a set of variables related to economic freedom, educational levels and the legal system, and reach the same conclusions.

According to Kugler and Feng, the existence of democratic institutions is also fundamental to promoting political stability, greater education, greater entrepreneurship and greater investment based on lower risk.

Tom Schuller explains that social capital, the maintenance of social cohesion, improves economic performance.[12] "Communication and teamwork skills are two of the most universally recognized competencies for a modern economy. They can be interpreted at a basic practical level, where productive efficiency requires good communication between work group members. But the same message applies at other levels, where a professional community depends for its health on trust and openness in the exchange of information, whether this is explicit or remains tacit.[13]

Defining social capital

The World Bank defines social capital as follows:

---

[10] Barro, Robert J. "Determinants Of Economic Growth:A Cross-Country Empirical Study" in *National Bureau of Economic Research*, 5698 (1996),   https://www.nber.org/system/files/working_papers/w5698/w5698.pdf.

[11] Nieswiadomy Michael L.; Strazicich, Mark C. "Are political freedoms converging?" in *Economic Inquiry*. 42, 2 (2004): 323-340.

[12] Ibid. pp. 4-5.

[13] Ibid. p. 17.

A society's social capital includes the institutions, relationships, attitudes and values that govern interactions between people and contribute to economic and social development. However, social capital is not simply the sum of the institutions that underpin society, but also the glue that holds them together. It includes the shared values and norms of social conduct expressed in personal relationships, trust and a common sense of "civic" responsibility that make society more than a collection of individuals. Without a degree of common identification with forms of government, cultural norms and social rules, it is difficult to imagine a functioning society.

The narrowest concept of social capital is associated with Putnam, who sees it as a set of "horizontal associations" between people: social capital consists of social networks ("civic engagement networks") and associated norms that have an effect on community productivity.

A second, broader concept of social capital was put forward by Coleman, who defines social capital as "a variety of different entities, with two elements in common: they all consist of some aspect of the social structure, and they all facilitate certain actions of actors - whether personal or corporate actors - within the structure." This definition broadens the concept to include both vertical and horizontal associations, and also behavior within and between other entities such as firms.

A third and most comprehensive view of social capital includes the social and political environment that shapes the social structure and enables the development of norms. In addition to the largely informal and often local horizontal and hierarchical relationships of the first two concepts, this view also includes the more formalized institutional relationships and structures, such as government, the political regime, the rule of law, the judicial system, and civil and political liberties. This focus on institutions is inspired by North and Olson, who have argued that such institutions have an important effect on the pace and pattern of economic development.[14]

Social capital generates reciprocity, trust, altruism, social norms, community, and resources such as information, knowledge, business opportunities, money, organizational resources, and emotional support.

Robert Putnam. Social capital fosters integration, cooperation, trust, and collective knowledge, which promote economic growth.

According to Robert Putnam, "Social capital refers to the connections between individuals: social networks and the norms of reciprocity and trust that arise from them. In this sense, social capital is closely related to what some have called "civic virtue".[15]

Social capital is a resource that promotes human well-being by fostering cooperation to solve collective problems. It promotes trust, which allows for more frequent interactions and reduced transaction costs. It promotes the creation of collective knowledge and awareness. It facilitates the achievement of community members' personal goals. Connectedness makes societies stronger and more integrated; it helps societies grow and expand.

---

[14] World Bank. *The Initiative on Defining, Monitoring and Measuring Social Capital. Overview and Program Description.* Washington, DC: The World Bank. 1998. pp. 1-2.

[15] Putnam, Robert D. *Bowling Alone. The Collapse and Revival of American Community.* New York. Simon & Schuster. 2000. p. 17.

For Putnam and Fukuyama, social capital reduces the transaction costs associated with coordination, such as contracts, rules, and their consequences: negotiations, monitoring, litigation, and enforcement.[16]

A culture of trust, a component of social capital, fosters economic growth.

Paul F. Whiteley[17] investigated the relationship between trust and GDP per capita in a sample of countries during 1992, showing a positive correlation. Trust has a positive impact on national intellectual capital, institutions and the success of political regimes. Additionally, trust has a positive impact on the microeconomy and organizations, as it reduces transaction costs between them.

Putnam demonstrates how, despite the same institutions throughout Italy, some areas possess more significant social capital and better functioning.

Francis Fukuyama believes that social capital is a prerequisite for a stable liberal democracy to promote cooperation in civic, economic, and political realities. Fukuyama postulates that trust is necessary for countries to prosper.

Authors Guiso, Sapienza and Zingales[18] confirm the link between culture and economic prosperity: a direct regression between confidence and economic performance; confidence has a positive impact and correlation

---

[16] Fukuyama, Francis. *Trust: The Social Virtues and the Creation of Prosperity*. New York. Simon and Schuster. 1996. p. 44.

[17] Whiteley, Paul F. "Economic Growth and Social Capital" in *Political Studies* 48, 3 (2000): 443-466. https://doi.org/10.1111/1467-9248.00269.

[18] Guiso, Luigi & Sapienza, Paola & Zingales, Luigi. "Does culture affect economic performance?" in *Journal of Economic Perspectives*. 20 (2006): 23-48. 10.2139/ssrn.876601.

with becoming an entrepreneur; a culture that values savings correlates positively with the national savings rate; culture influences political and institutional preferences and, consequently, behavior and outcomes; culture and religion influence attitudes toward hard work, redistribution and welfare governance; culture influences the belief that poverty is the fault of society rather than the individual's effort; culture influences social capital, which impacts social organizations, such as health and education; culture influences attitudes toward "autonomy, egalitarianism, leading to greater rule of law, less corruption and more democratic accountability"; "Trust, belief in the importance of personal effort, widespread morality and low obedience" are positively correlated with the effectiveness of institutions and, consequently, with wealth and economic growth.[19]

Daron Acemoglu and Matthew O. Jackson[20] draw on game theory to demonstrate how culture and history influence social cooperation. In other words, past behavior encourages expected behavior, but changes when leadership introduces new cues, expectations and norms.

Alberto Alesina and Paola Giuliano conclude that, "Culture and institutions interact and evolve in a complementary way, with mutual feedback effects."[21]

---

[19] Ibid.

[20] Acemoglu, Daron; Jackson Matthew O. "History, Expectations and Leadership in the Evolution of Cooperation." in *Journal of Economic Studies.* 2011. http://www.dklevine.com/archive/refs4786969000000000106.pdf

[21] Alesina, Alberto and Paola Giuliano. "Culture and Institutions" in *Journal of Economic Literature,* 53 (4) (2015): 898-944. DOI: 10.1257/jel.53.4.898, p. 938.

Guido Tabellini[22] measures culture through indicators of personal values and beliefs, such as trust and respect for others and confidence in one's
own self-determination. Analyzing Europe, he finds that "the most backward regions (with higher illiteracy rates and worse political institutions)
tend to exhibit specific cultural traits today: less generalized trust, less respect for others, and less trust in the individual. Less trust and respect for
others and less trust in the individual are associated with lower per capita
output and slower growth rates.[23]

According to Tabellini, autocratic and corrupt regimes demand an ar-
bitrary distribution of privileges and the use of force, fostering distrust, im-
potence and resignation. On the opposite side, a democratic culture fosters
trust, entrepreneurship, investment, a strong work ethic that encourages
productivity, support of institutions and widespread morale. This reinforces positive cultural values based on role models: a culture that fosters
general morality leads to economic growth.

Douglass North and institutions

According to Douglass North[24] institutions are necessary to reduce
transaction costs: "man-made constraints that structure political, economic and social interactions". North compares the poor quality of institutions in developing countries as manifested in poorly framed property
rights and inefficient operations and markets. These factors raise

---

[22] Tabellini, Guido. "Culture and Institutions: Economic Development
in the Regions of Europe," in *Journal of the European Economic Association*
8, 4, (2010): 677-716, https://doi.org/10.1111/j.1542-4774.2010.tb00537.x.

[23] Ibid. p. 3.

[24] North, Douglass C. *Transaction Costs, Institutions and Economic
Performance*. San Francisco. International Center for Economic Growth.
1992.

transaction costs and discourage investors from investing in new ventures: higher information costs to manage more complex contracts, higher law enforcement costs, bribery and corruption costs, and higher transformation costs can make investment unprofitable or prohibitive.

According to North[25] markets increase transaction costs; institutions reduce them by controlling socially harmful behavior. North identifies several transaction costs: agency, information asymmetry between the parties to the exchange, contract enforcement, and differing ideologies. "Transaction costs arise because information is costly and asymmetric for the parties to the exchange." The role of political, economic and legal institutions is to reduce these transaction costs by controlling socially harmful behavior.[26]

As North argues, a fundamental element of the institutional arrangement is the organizations and the entrepreneurs within them: "If the institutions are the rules of the game, the organizations are the players". [27] North believes in a minimal state: "If the state has coercive force, those who run the state will use that force in their own self-interest at the expense of the rest of society."[28]

Statistical evidence that institutions foster economic growth

There is abundant research demonstrating the positive correlation between economic growth and institutions.

---

[25] Ibid.

[26] Ibid. p. 8.

[27] Ibid. p. 7.

[28] North, Douglass C. *Institutions, Institutional Change, and Economic Performance*. Cambridge University Press. New York. 1990. p. 58.

Dani Rodrik, Arvind Subramanian and Francesco Trebbi[29] analyze the factors that influence GDP per capita: institutions, geographic location and economic integration with other countries. The results show the significant prevalence of institutions over geography and economic integration.

Edwin Feulner[30] correlates economic growth with institutions as re-flected in three indicators: property rights, absence of corruption and rule of law, showing that GDP is strongly correlated with institutions. Feulner correlates the rule of law index with the inflow of foreign investment and with the unemployment rate, confirming that institutions are good for business.

---

[29] Rodrik, Dani; Subramanian, Arvind; Trebbi, Francesco. "Institutions Rule: The Primacy of Institutions Over Geography and Integration in Economic Development" in *Journal of Economic Growth* 9 (2004): 131-165.

[30] Feulner, Edwin. "The Rule of Law" in *Index of Economic Freedom*. Washington, DC. The Heritage Foundation. 2013.

Chapter 3

Social Justice is Based on Resources

According to the United Nations, the well-being of citizens requires economic growth and social justice:

> The well-being of citizens requires broad-based and sustainable economic growth, economic justice, the provision of employment opportunities and, more generally, the existence of conditions for the optimal development of people as individuals and social beings.
>
> Social justice can be broadly understood as the fair and compassionate distribution of the fruits of economic growth; however, some important qualifiers need to be added to this statement. Today, maximizing growth seems to be the primary objective, but it is also essential to ensure that growth is sustainable, that the integrity of the natural environment is respected, that the use of non-renewable resources is rationalized, and that future generations can enjoy a beautiful and hospitable earth. The conception of social justice must integrate these dimensions, starting with the right of all human beings to benefit from a safe and pleasant environment, which implies the equitable sharing among countries and social groups of the cost of environmental protection and of the development of safe technologies for production and safe products for consumption.[1]

---

[1] The International Forum for Social Development. *Social justice in an open world. The role of the United Nations.* United Nations Department of Economic and Social Affairs. 2006

Social justice has a positive impact on economic growth

Anil Savio Kavuri and Hongwei Shao find that social justice is a prerequisite for economic growth, as social justice "influences technology, labor and capital, which in turn affect economic performance [...] Simple OLS regressions illustrate that, for OECD countries, a 1-point increase in the weighted index of social justice would increase GDP per capita by 61% when controlling for endogeneity.[2]

---

[2] Kavuri, Anil Savio and Hongwei Shao. *The Impact of Social Justice on Economic Performance.* Australia. Crawford School of Public Policy. Center for Applied Macroeconomic Analysis. 2017. p. 5.

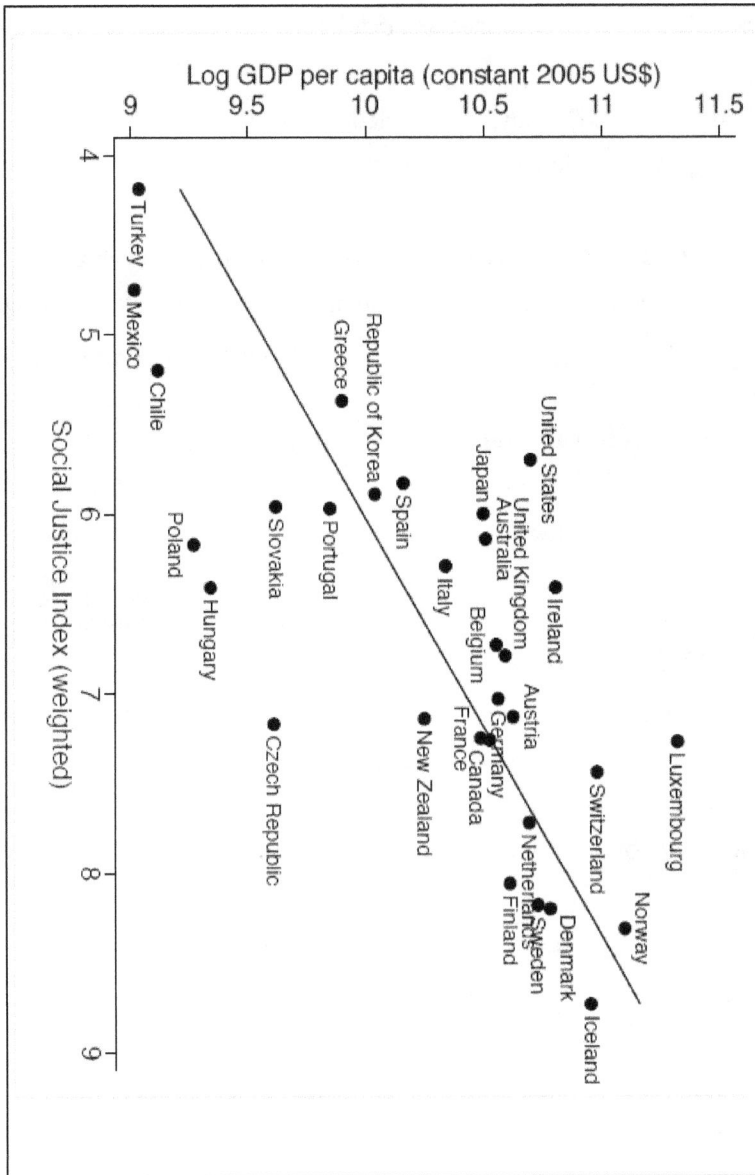

Figure 28 Correlation between wealth and social justice. Kavuri, Anil Savio, and Hongwei Shao. *The Impact of Social Justice on Economic Performance*. Crawford School of Public Policy. Centre for Applied Macroeconomic Analysis. Australia. 2017. p. 5.

Economic growth increases as equality rises

Roberto Perotti[3] analyzes the relationship between income distribution and growth, reviewing the main theories that study this relationship.

- **Fiscal policies**: growth increases as distortionary taxation decreases; redistributive public spending and thus distortionary taxation decrease as equality increases; **growth increases as equality increases**.[4]
- **Sociopolitical instability.** Investment and growth increase as socio-political instability decreases; socio-political instability decreases as equality increases; **growth increases as equality increases**.[5]
- **Imperfect capital markets.** Growth increases as investment in human capital increases; for any degree of capital market imperfection, investment in human capital increases as **equality** increases; **growth increases as equality increases**.[6]

Economic growth can have a positive impact on social justice

Douglas Voigt argues that growth expands people's choices and enhances social justice: "Social policy combining income support and active prevention and integration measures not only fosters citizens' financial self-sufficiency, but also their autonomy in terms of "human flourishing", which is critically based on what Amartya Sen and Martha Nussbaum have

---

[3] Perotti, Roberto. "Growth, Income Distribution and Democracy: What the Data " in *Journal of Economic Growth* 1, 2 (1996): 149-187. p. 5.

[4] Ibid. p. 3.

[5] Ibid. p. 4.

[6] Ibid.

called the "capabilities" given to people and social relations to enhance well-being [....] a complementary relationship between this labor market supply policy and economic growth that results in greater social justice.[7] High-growth environments effectively subsidize low-growth environments (by less within Germany), resulting in the migration of those seeking upward social mobility or those who are young and rootless enough to be "activated" in a higher-growth region.[8]

Solidarity requires resources

Jeffrey Sachs[9] believes that extreme poverty (people earning less than a dollar a day) can be eliminated if richer countries provide some primary capital to the poor to help them out of the poverty trap. According to Sachs, a "poverty trap" exists. It occurs when extreme poverty blocks all avenues of economic growth.

For Sachs, the more advantaged countries should help the disadvantaged to develop capital, in terms of

- Human capital: health, nutrition and skills necessary for each person to be economically productive.
- Business capital: machinery, plant and motorized transport used in agriculture, industry and services.

---

[7] Voigt, Douglas. "Economic Growth and Social Justice: Testing a Third Way Assumption on the German Case" in *DFG-KollegforscherInnengruppe Postwachstumsgesellschaften.* 2016. p. 1.

[8] Ibid. p. 2.

[9] Sachs, Jeffrey. *The End of Poverty: Economic Possibilities for Our Time.* Penguin Press. 2005.

- Infrastructure: roads, energy, water and sanitation, airports and seaports, and telecommunications systems, which are key inputs for business productivity.
- Natural capital: arable land, healthy soils, biodiversity and well-functioning ecosystems that provide the environmental services needed by human society.
- Public institutional capital: commercial law, judicial systems, government services and police that support the peaceful and prosperous division of labor.
- Knowledge capital: scientific and technological knowledge that increases the productivity of business production and the development of physical and natural capital.[10]

Following this approach, the United Nations established the Millennium Development Goals, to be achieved by 2015: 1. Eradicate extreme poverty and hunger; 2. Achieve universal primary education; 3. Promote gender equality and empower women; 4. Reduce child mortality; 5. Improve maternal health; 6. Combat HIV/AIDS, malaria and other diseases; 7. Ensure environmental sustainability; 8. Develop a global partnership for development.[11]

According to *The Guardian*, the Program was quite successful: "total lives saved between 2000-2015: 29.7 million; 471 million have been lifted out of extreme poverty; lower-income countries accelerated in sanitation, water, maternal mortality, child mortality."[12]

---

[10] Ibid. pp. 244-245.

[11] https://www.un.org/millenniumgoals/

[12]The Guardian. *Results of the Millennium Development Agenda. How successful have the Millennium Development Goals been?*, https://www.the-guardian.com/global-development-professionals-net-work/2017/mar/30/how-successful-were-the-millennium-development-

In 2015, the goals were partially achieved, so the group launched a new set of goals, the Sustainable Development Goals for 2030: 1. No poverty; 2. Zero hunger; 3. Good health and well-being for people; 4. Quality education; 5. Gender equality; 6. Clean water and sanitation; 7. Affordable and clean energy; 8. Decent work and economic growth; 9. Industry, innovation and infrastructure; 10. Reducing inequalities; 11. Sustainable cities and communities; 12. Responsible consumption and production; 13.[13]

Subsidiarity requires resources

The United Nations, Community legislation and the Maastricht Treaty uphold the principle of subsidiarity: what individuals can achieve through their initiative and effort should not be taken away from them by a higher authority.

Vaclav Havel, along with Desmond Tutu and the Dalai Lama, among others, has been a strong advocate of the necessity and value of civil societies, in which citizens actively participate, while the state is limited to its sole tasks: law, security, and defense.[14]

William Russell Easterly questions the impact of international aid for several reasons. He states, for example, that the free nets provided by foreign aid to protect against malaria "are often diverted to the black market,

---

goals https://www.theguardian.com/global-development/millennium-development-goals

[13] https://www.undp.org/content/undp/en/home/sustainable-development-goals.html

[14] Havel, Vaclav. *Vaclav Havel's ideas and his conception of Civil Society.* Speech by Vaclav Havel, President of the Czech Republic, on the occasion of the Vaclav Havel Civil Society Symposium, April 26, 1999, https://eng.yabloko.ru/Publ/Archive/Speech/gavel-260499.html.

fail to reach health clinics, or end up being used as fishing nets or wedding veils [...] In Zambia, 70% of beneficiaries did not use the nets."[15]

Easterly criticizes Sachs' approach, arguing that aid agencies often lack feedback and accountability, which makes their operations inefficient. India and China produced economic growth and social justice based on their own efforts and free markets.

Amartya Sen: resources for operation.

According to Amartya Sen, a person needs to be able to function to achieve well-being, and this requires specific capabilities for functioning.[16]

Sen describes "functioning" in two dimensions: "being" (being well nourished, living in a good environment, having specific abilities or disabilities, physical and emotional health, having a good education and the ability to adapt to reality) and "doing" (working, studying, speaking, traveling, voting, eating).

These capabilities provide freedom to pursue diverse lifestyles, promote personal initiative, and personal agency.

Sen's capabilities approach focuses on human welfare and human development, rather than solely on the economy, assigning each person a central role according to their capabilities. Sen sums it up this way: "To better understand the role of human capabilities, we must take into account their direct importance for people's well-being and freedom, their

---

[15] Easterly, William Russell. *The White Man's Burden: Why the West's Efforts to Aid the Rest Have Done So Much Ill and So Little Good.* London. Penguin Books. 2006. p. 23.

[16] Ibid. p. 75.

indirect role in influencing economic production, and their indirect role in influencing social change."[17]

Subsidiarity, civil economy, and social capital.

Luigino Bruni and Stefano Zamagni defend the civil economy perspective, the role of the State in social welfare is that of initiator, planner and regulator, but not necessarily that of executor, which depends on other factors such as its economic efficiency:

> The civil economy paradigm teaches that market trade is not merely an impersonal exchange, but also an exercise of the civil virtues [...] Market exchange can build social solidarity when buyers and sellers recognize and embrace the moral foundations of mutually beneficial trade [....] For the school of civil economy, the market, the enterprise, the economy are themselves the place of friendship, reciprocity, gratuitousness and fraternity [...] The economy is civil, the market is life in common, and they share the same fundamental law: mutual aid [...] Note the difference between exchange and mutual aid. In an act of exchange, each party benefits from a transaction that is only possible because it benefits the other. However, neither party should be concerned with the interests of the other. Mutual aid implies more than this. It implies the intention, on the part of the person assisting, to benefit the person assisted. If the assistance is mutual, these intentions are reciprocal. [18]

Healthy economies are based on an anthropology of "trust," "mutual advantage" and "happiness" that emphasizes "reciprocity,

---

[17] Sen, Amartya. *Human Capital and Human Capability. World Development.* Amsterdam. Elsevier Science. 1997. p. 2.

[18] Ibid.

friendship and mutual assistance or fraternity" as the essence of production and exchange.[19]

Reward is the necessary link to bind particular interest to general interest, and to keep men always oriented towards the good [...] Civil economy is an attempt to train [people] to be "sincerely" virtue-loving, to attribute to it also an intrinsic value, based on the attempt to show them that virtue, especially when it is reciprocal has its own logic, a rationality. [20]

---

[19] Bruni, Luigino and Stefano Zamagni. *The civil economy. Another idea of the market*. Editorial Agenda. 2016. United Kingdom.

[20] Bruni, Luigino. *Il Contributo italiano alla storia del Pensiero*. Economia. 2012.

Part 3

A Great Leadership

Introduction

This Part 3 extends the CAPSTONE, incorporating leadership to maximize the welfare of society.

Part 1 showed that to create economic value, organizations must satisfy their customers better than the competition, grow more than others, and manage their resources better. In other words, economic value creation demands great leadership, it demands excellence.

This Part 3 presents a new conception of leadership as a process, enriched by the Baldrige Excellence Framework, its values and its structure to promote great leadership, to produce the best results for society.

This prepares Module 2 of this book "Decision making with discernment", which analyzes how discernment promotes a culture of leadership.

Chapter 1

Leaders maximize intellectual capital

Leaders contribute to and maximize the intellectual capital components of an organization or nation.

- **Leaders contribute human capital** because they help build better knowledge, wisdom, information, ideas, because they foster research, creativity, innovation, entrepreneurship, development of competencies, skills, organizational knowledge, labor productivity, dialogue, social and personality attributes, values, motivation, interdisciplinary science, education, health and life expectancy.

  Leaders promote better organizational knowledge, awareness, humanism, sharing experiences, integrating diverse sources of knowledge, thus fostering creativity, the discovery of new ideas and meanings.

  Human capital is part of intellectual capital, promoting the economic value of a company expressed in the MVA (Market Value Added).

- **Leaders provide social capital.** Leaders promote empathy (Edith Stein), effective teams (Jon Katzenbach), organizations as organisms and networks (Gareth Morgan), strategic alliances (Torger Reeve), and emotional intelligence (Daniel Goleman).

  Leaders provide social capital because they create relationships, social networks, norms of reciprocity, goodwill, supportive institutions and culture, things that generate collaboration and trust.

Leaders provide social capital because they promote an institutionalist vision: companies must be good citizens to be successful and promote personal and community values to be accepted and rewarded by all stakeholders.

Leaders provide social capital by supporting culture, engendering collaboration and trust; leaders provide shared values and norms of social behavior expressed in personal relationships and vertical and horizontal partnerships; leaders provide a shared sense of civic responsibility, shared social norms, a sense of community, reciprocity, mutually beneficial cooperation, altruism and emotional support; leaders provide cultural values that influence decisions, promote entrepreneurship and frugality. Leadership promotes attitudes toward hard work, welfare, health care, education, rule of law, responsibility, personal effort, ethics, reduction of free riding, and efficiency of institutions.

In the prisoner's dilemma model of game theory, if the first player believes that the second player will act with leadership, then he will act with leadership, as will the rest of society. This is true in all dimensions of political economy: the leadership of some people will encourage others to change their behavior and act with leadership as well.

Leaders provide social capital by reducing transaction costs, minimizing the agency problem, reducing information asymmetry, reducing the cost of information, reducing law enforcement costs, reducing costs arising from bribery and corruption, and reducing the cost of transformation, thereby increasing the return on investment, which leads to promoting investment, social entrepreneurship, social innovation, social change, business opportunities, growth and prosperity.

Leaders promote a culture that welcomes investors, fosters goodwill, civic and political freedoms, internationality, commercial intensity, social and educational equality, knowledge sharing and organizational resources.

Social capital is part of intellectual capital, the economic value of a company expressed in the FMV.

- **Leaders provide Structural Capital.** They promote wisdom, transcendence, the creation of goodness, beauty, truth, higher values, greatness, altruism, discernment, meaning in life, the ability to face suffering and the power to transform and heal; they foster social action, which enhances entrepreneurship.

    A leader acts with discernment, relying on the knowledge created and shared among stakeholders. That is why decision-making is characterized by social sensitivity. That is: each member of society is valued, the best is sought for all parties, and intellectual capital, knowledge and relationships are maximized. Discernment goes beyond critical thinking, because it involves resources that go beyond those of the intellect: personal and community knowledge, transcendence, values, relationships and the meaning of life.

    Leaders turn organizations into agents of transformation. They transform themselves, they transform the community, they transform the world. They create higher realities: innovation, entrepreneurship, growth, continuous improvement. In a word, they build a better society, a better world.

    Leaders promote continuous improvement processes in organizations because they consider the organization as part of a system: The balanced scorecard developed by Norton and Kaplan, the Baldrige National Quality Award, and Deming's Total Quality Management, all reflect this systemic view of the organization's continuous improvement processes, in which economic value increases along with stakeholder satisfaction.

Structural Capital is part of the intellectual capital, of the economic value of a company expressed in the MVA. Our leadership encourages the execution of social actions, social change and the empowerment of intellectual capital.

- **Leaders transform business ethics** which manifests itself in various dimensions of ethics:

In the cognitive dimension, where prudence, wisdom, mental clarity, emotional awareness, judgment, learning capacity, richer personal and community knowledge play a prominent role. All this illuminated by meditation, contemplation, the construction of personal authenticity, the improvement of consequentialism proper to utilitarianism, the improvement of the criteria of idealistic normative ethics.

In the transcendental dimension, which is manifested in the valuation and construction of transcendence, goodness, beauty, truth, love and the "participation" of creatures in the perfections of the creator (for believers or religious people).

In the axiological dimension, which proposes an ethics based on values, promoting conscience, knowledge and intellectual virtues such as prudence, wisdom, perceptions and feelings. Max Scheler proposes, in this respect, a rank or hierarchy of values, where right, aesthetics and truth are prioritized. Values lead people and organizations to change their behaviors, build virtues and maximize happiness. Values foster personal and social transformation.

In the relational dimension, which fosters an ethical community and reciprocity. Scheler's ranges of values prioritize justice, social inclusion, cooperation, solidarity, working for the common good, pacification, harmonization, an end to crime and abuses of power and economic resources.

In the execution of ethics, where motivation and energy, emotional control and the ability to communicate, understand and interact with people create a better reality. Leaders foster a social ethic that promotes human dignity, the value of the person, the sanctity of human life, human rights and property rights; the dignity of the family, community and participation; the dignity of work and respect for the worker; solidarity, social justice, the pursuit of the common good, the role of government in ensuring the common good; subsidiarity, intermediate organizations; care for creation. This is a social ethic based on communitarian, relational values and affection, which help to develop virtues and community-oriented behaviors.

- **Leaders transform** value-based **corporate social responsibility**, such as employee welfare, profit sharing and trust management.

   They promote an institutionalist view of corporate social responsibility. The stakeholder model (Edward Freeman, Stakeholder Theory), for example, contributes to the harmony of all stakeholders, and that of corporate citizenship (Corporate Citizenship) to the organization's identity as part of the community. Employee welfare and paternalism reinforce employee loyalty to the organization. Corporate Social Performance is based on mechanisms that align the entire organization, its resources and processes behind social issues. The Corporate Social Responsiveness model focuses on how organizations actively engage and interact with communities to improve the quality of life and the environment. Consumer Based CSR has beneficial effects on customers and the image and perception of companies, philanthropy promotes social change.

The leaders promote an institutionalist view of CSR in several ways. Firstly, taking into account the Three Domain CSR approach, which involves three institutional dimensions: economic (responsibility for the global economy), legal (responsibility for shareholders) and ethical (responsibility for stakeholders). Secondly, considering that corporate social performance involves three other institutional dimensions: institutional (legitimacy), organizational (public accountability) and personal (managerial discretion). Thirdly, by promoting community-oriented processes: environmental assessment, adaptation of the organization to the environment, stakeholder and problem management, stakeholder participation and communication, and results of corporate behaviors, such as social impacts, social programs, social policies. Finally, they promote an institutionalist view of corporate social responsibility because they encourage socially responsible investment and corporate citizenship, promoting companies as stewards of citizens' rights, such as social, political and civil rights, together with government and civic organizations.

Chapter 2

Leadership as an organizational resource: leadership as a process

There are multiple models of leadership.

To mention the best known ones: Autocratic (the leader decides), Democratic / Participative (involves followers), Transformational (inspires and motivates by creating a vision of the future), Transactional (rewards and punishments), Laissez-Faire (gives autonomy), Servant (prioritizes the well-being of his team members), Charismatic (trusts the leader's personality), Situational (adapts to reality), Coaching (develops his team's skills), Visionary (thinks ahead), Commanding (directs and controls the team), Pacesetting (to achieve challenging objectives), Collaborative (teamwork, shared decision-making), Intercultural (relevant in international or multicultural environments), Delegative (distributes authority), Innovative (prioritizes creativity), Ethical (prioritizes integrity, transparency and morality), Strategic (sets long-term goals, provides resources), and the list goes on and on.

This chapter presents a process-based view of leadership, which has several advantages:

- It is a resource of the organization; it does not depend on a person like autocratic leadership, charismatic leadership, coaching, command, among others.
- It integrates several of the most important leadership styles just listed: transformational, democratic, strategic, visionary, situational, ethical, innovative, among others.

111

- It emerges from the ten dimensions of discernment that we will see in the book "A new Capstone - Decision making with discernment": it is born from the best organizational knowledge, it seeks transcendence, it is based on values, it integrates the community, it makes decisions incorporating the person and the community, it is transforming, healing, and it seeks the good of the community.

The concept of "processes" emerged during the reengineering of a couple of decades ago as the best way to integrate functions and create micro-organizations, teams focused on specific processes.

Some key processes emerged, such as new product development or customer service, which forced the integration of certain functions, making them work as a team, with autonomy, to ensure a fast and successful performance. For example, developing a new product within the traditional organizational structure, which was structured by function, could take two years, as each unit completed its role before involving the next unit. Meanwhile, in Asia, companies were launching new products in six months. From there, they started to create units organized by process, involving all required functions, working simultaneously, ensuring that a new product could be created in six months.

There are multiple definitions of leadership that converge in that leadership is a process, a resource, a competence.

According to Bickes and Yilmaz "Leadership is the process of facilitating individual and collective efforts and influencing others to achieve common goals."[1]

Bernard Bass presents the vision of leadership as a process:

---

[1] Bickes, D. Mehmet; Yilmaz, Celal. *Leadership Theories. A Handbook of Leadership Styles.* Newcastle upon Tyne. Cambridge Scholars Publishing. 2020. p 1.

This definition of leadership as a process is gaining increasing popularity. Yukl (1994) defines leadership in organizations as a set of processes, including influencing others, interpreting events for followers, setting goals for the group or organization, organizing work to achieve these goals, motivating followers to achieve these goals, maintaining cooperative relationships and teamwork, and recruiting outsiders to support and cooperate with the group or organization.[2]

Alvesson goes a step further in understanding leadership as a process, highlighting the interaction between leadership and organizational culture:

Organizational culture is a primary focus of academic research and training in organizational theory, as well as management practice. There are good reasons for this: the cultural dimension is central to all aspects of organizational life.

Culture is thus a central element in the understanding of behavior, social events, institutions and processes. It refers to the environment in which these phenomena become understandable and meaningful. Culture is seen as a more or less cohesive system of meanings and symbols in terms of which social interaction takes place, while by social structure we mean those patterns of behavior to which social interaction itself gives rise. In the case of culture, then, we have a frame of reference of beliefs, expressive symbols and values through which individuals define their environment, express their feelings and make

---

[2] Bass, Bernard M.; Bass, Ruth. The Bass Handbook of Leadership. Theory, research, and managerial applications. Fourth Edition. Free Press. 2008. p 41.

judgments. In the latter case, i.e., at the social level, we have a continuous process of interaction.[3]

[3] Alvesson, Mats. *Leadership and Organizational Culture. The SAGE Handbook of Leadership*. SAGE Publications. 2011. p 153.

Chapter 3

Leadership Capabilities as a Process

Leadership is a process, that is, a set of capabilities acting together, that individuals or communities have, to lead the members of an organization towards certain objectives.

1. The ability to create a vision for the future of society that promotes transcendence, goodness, beauty, and truth.

The vision refers to a future ideal that may remain an ideal for many years, perhaps forever.

There is a universal consensus that leaders create a vision and can motivate others to work towards that goal.[1]

2. The ability to build missions, values, purpose, identity, commitment, and a role in society.

While the vision speaks of a future ideal, the mission situates us in the present, in how we walk towards that ideal, in what our commitment to it is, and what our values are.

The word mission refers to a person who wants to transform the world, who wants to do something valuable for it, and who is willing to move towards an ideal world.

Many authors agree that vision should inspire missions, influence, and motivate others:

---

[1] https://www.techtarget.com/searchcio/definition/leadership

- "Leadership is the art of motivating a group of people to act toward the achievement of a common goal."[2]
- "Leadership is a process of social influence that maximizes the efforts of others toward the achievement of a goal."[3]
- "Leadership builds a sense of belonging, shapes culture."[4]

3. The ability to build communities and relationships that promote social engagement.

Within the modern understanding of leadership, a leader is conceived as a person capable of transforming, through communication, motivation, and training, other people into leaders throughout the organization to help develop its vision and mission.

Several authors propose definitions that highlight the central role of the leader in building community and relationships where vision and mission are shared:

- "Leadership is about helping people succeed, inspiring and uniting people behind a common purpose and then being accountable."[5]

---

[2] https://www.thebalancesmb.com/leadership-definition-2948275

[3] https://www.forbes.com/sites/kevinkruse/2013/04/09/what-is-leadership/?sh=369521015b90

[4] https://holdsworthcenter.org/blog/leadership-definition-is-game-changer/?gclid=Cj0KCQjwuMuRBhCJARIsAHXdnqPzVB78op-HjFrHOEWOfZKvjJN9Hx2CtYWg78AfLr5aI4CKrlfhZA-qcaAn_QEALw_wcB

[5] https://medium.com/jacob-morgan/14-top-ceos-share-their-definition-of-leadership-whats-yours-2b89a58576a6

- "Leadership is the ability to inspire a team to achieve a certain goal."[6]
- "Leadership is the ability of an individual or group of individuals to influence and guide followers or other members of an organization."[7]
- "Leadership is influence, no more, no less."[8]
- "Looking ahead to the next century, leaders will be those who empower others."[9]
- "Leadership is about helping others realize their potential and inspiring them to work with you to achieve a shared vision for the future[10]
- "Leaders align talent systems."[11]
- "Leaders listen, equip others, appreciate them, help them develop, coach them, develop relationships, and serve their team members."[12]

---

[6] https://www.tonyrobbins.com/what-is-leadership/

[7] https://extension.sdstate.edu/what-definition-leadership

[8] https://www.forbes.com/sites/kevinkruse/2013/04/09/what-is-leadership/?sh=369521015b90

[9] https://www.forbes.com/sites/kevinkruse/2013/04/09/what-is-leadership/?sh=369521015b90

[10] https://medium.com/jacob-morgan/14-top-ceos-share-their-definition-of-leadership-whats-yours-2b89a58576a6

[11] https://holdsworthcenter.org/blog/leadership-definition-is-game-changer/?gclid=Cj0KCQjwuMuRBhCJARIsAHXdnqPzVB78op-HjFrHOEWOfZKvjJN9Hx2CtYWg78AfLr5aI4CKrlfhZA-qcaAn_QEALw_wcB"

[12] https://nlctb.org/tips/7-traits-of-emotionally-intelligent-leaders/?gclid=Cj0KCQjwuMuRBhCJARI-sAHXdnqPCTu5v6rrh4tWVRVz2SOtk-IpFP-Zx9HFRDZ_opGEzIl-PwXgIEgxMaAsnFEALw_wcB

4. The ability to make meaningful decisions based on discernment.

Decision-making involves determining how an organization can define its objectives, strategies, required resources, and expected outcomes to transform the ideal into reality.

Strategic management is based on the ability to analyze the system, the environment, the strategies, the results and establish the rational connection between them to ensure the success of the organization.

This is a core competency of a leader: "The most basic definition of leadership is that you set the destination. You devise a strategy to get to that destination and you do everything you can to align and supply the resources to make that happen."[13]

5. The capacity to transform, heal, execute social actions and drive social change.

As defined by some authors:

- "Leadership is the ability to translate vision into reality."[14]
- "I define leadership as having a positive impact on people; employees, shareholders, customers, business partners and the general public."[15]

---

13   https://medium.com/jacob-morgan/14-top-ceos-share-their-definition-of-leadership-whats-yours-2b89a58576a6

14   https://www.forbes.com/sites/kevinkruse/2013/04/09/what-is-leadership/?sh=369521015b90

15   https://medium.com/jacob-morgan/14-top-ceos-share-their-definition-of-leadership-whats-yours-2b89a58576a6

- "Make bold goal setting a core belief. Do things, as John F. Kennedy said, 'not because they are easy, but because they are hard.'"[16]
- "Leadership is synonymous with progress, empowerment, empathy and trust. In an age of too many cynics throwing up their hands and shouting "impossible," I employ optimism, the only free encouragement in this world."[17]

---

[16] https://medium.com/jacob-morgan/14-top-ceos-share-their-definition-of-leadership-whats-yours-2b89a58576a6

[17] https://medium.com/jacob-morgan/14-top-ceos-share-their-definition-of-leadership-whats-yours-2b89a58576a6

Chapter 4

Leadership as a process proposed by the Baldrige Excellence Framework

Leadership is an overused word, even in low-level issues. In this book, we are looking for great leadership. What does greatness mean?

Greatness refers to the dimensions, size and degree of something. The greatness of a person refers to the dimensions of a person, taking into account his or her being, soul, spirit, nature, faculties, personality, emotions, resources, skills, abilities, power, decisions, actions, behaviors, virtues, ethics, and results.

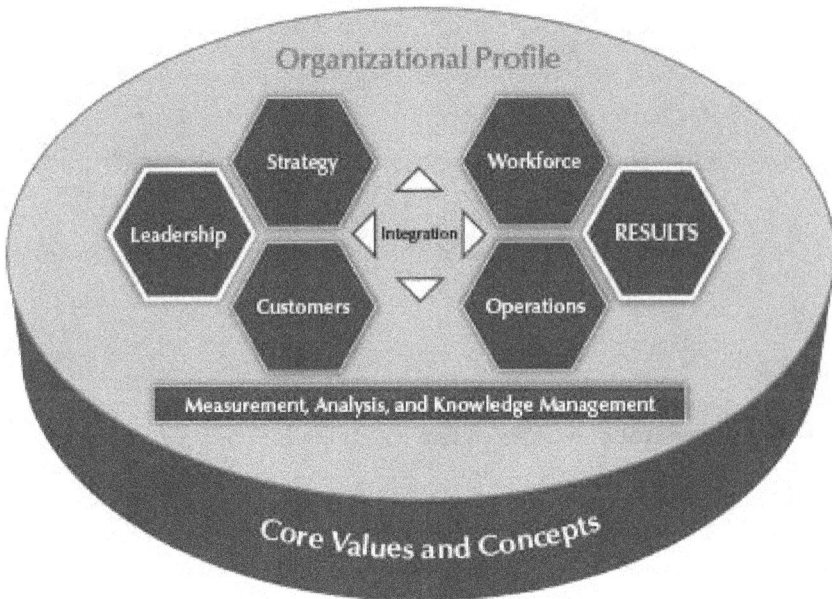

To analyze how to build leadership with greatness, we will rely on the prestigious Baldrige Performance Excellence Program[1] . Along with other similar programs in other countries, it promotes excellence, helps organizations to fulfill their mission, improve their results and become more competitive.

The Baldrige Excellence Framework includes the Criteria for Performance Excellence, core values and concepts, and guidelines to assess your processes and results, help you innovate and improve.

The reader can see that the five capabilities described in the leadership by process outlined above are aligned with the process outlined by the Baldrige Excellence Framework:

1. The ability to create a vision for the future of society that promotes transcendence.
2. The ability to build missions, values, purpose, identity, commitment, and a role in society.
3. The ability to build communities and relationships, which promote social engagement.
4. The ability to make meaningful decisions based on discernment.
5. The capacity to transform, heal, execute social actions, and drive social change.

The fundamental concepts of the Baldrige Excellence Framework

Baldrige Excellence Framework is a continuous and sustainable improvement approach that aims to promote innovation and excellence in all areas of the organization. The continuous improvement system involves constant:

---

[1] https://www.nist.gov/baldrige/publications/baldrige-excellence-framework

- Self-Assessment. Organizations can utilize the Baldrige criteria to conduct a self-assessment, identifying strengths and areas for improvement.
- Benchmarking. It compares performance with that of other organizations in the same industry using the Baldrige framework.
- Continuous improvement plan. Develops a plan to address identified deficiencies and implement improvements based on the results of the assessment.

It is based on the "Total Quality" management philosophy, based on continuous improvement, proposed by Edward Deming, the creator of Total Quality Management (TQM).

TQM has as its antecedent process reengineering, which proposed to improve quality, changing the paradigm of organizational structures based on functions, towards organizations by processes, which group functions, to gain in efficiency, speed, communication, and agility in decision making. Reengineering promotes work teams that incorporate functions to process organizations, such as new product development, which reduces the time from two years to six months to launch a new product. Customer service also incorporates functions to ensure excellent and agile service, among other benefits.

Reengineering proposes drastic changes generated from the top of the organization. In contrast, TQM proposes continuous improvements in a sustained and gradual way, which emerge from the organization itself, systemically.

The Baldrige Model is fundamentally based on Total Quality Management, promoting an organizational process of continuous improvement toward excellence.

It proposes four factors for evaluating the process: focus, deployment, learning, and integration, which lead to continuous improvement toward excellence. These factors are crucial in the discernment we will discuss in the book "A new Capstone - Decision making with discernment".

Baldrige Excellence Framework Values

The Baldrige Excellence Framework is based on the following core values: visionary leadership, organizational learning and agility, customer-oriented excellence, valuing people, focus on social results, ethical behavior, managing for innovation, systems perspective, results orientation and value creation, transparency, and focus on success.

Performance Excellence Criteria

The Criteria are the foundation of the program. These Criteria provide a detailed set of guidelines that organizations can use to evaluate their performance in different aspects.

1. Leadership.

How leaders guide the organization, create a culture of excellence, and focus on customer needs. Baldrige expands the leadership process, incorporating other processes that lead the organization to continuous improvement.

2. Strategy: development and implementation.

How the organization develops and implements its strategy, ensuring alignment with its mission and vision

The Baldrige Framework emphasizes three key aspects of organizational excellence that are important for strategic planning:

- **Customer-focused excellence** is a strategic vision of excellence.
- **Improved operational performance and innovation** contribute to both short-term and long-term productivity growth, as well as cost and price competitiveness.
- **Organizational learning and staff learning** are strategic considerations in today's challenging environment.

Excellence, improvement, and learning lead to greatness.

Strategy and decision making are at the heart of the discernment we will discuss in the book "A new Capstone - Decision making with discernment".

3. Customers: listening to them, satisfying them, creating relationships.

How the organization focuses on understanding and meeting customer needs, and building lasting relationships. That mechanism of listening and awareness of customer realities will be the first chapter we will discuss in Volume 2. How to build relationships and communities will be the fifth chapter of the book "A new Capstone - Decision making with discernment".

4. Measurement, analysis, review, improvement of organizational performance, and knowledge management.

How the organization uses data and information to make decisions and manage performance. The first chapter of the book "A new Capstone - Decision making with discernment" delves into knowledge creation and management.

5. Staff

How the organization engages and develops its people, ensuring a motivated, high-performing team. The third chapter of the book "A new Capstone - Decision making with discernment" delves into how to create a culture of motivation and high performance.

6. Operations and processes

How the organization designs, manages and improves its processes to achieve better results

7. Results

How the organization monitors and evaluates its performance results in various areas, products and processes, customer satisfaction, financial performance and employee engagement. The results consider four factors that are very valuable in our discernment work:

- **Levels** are the actual performance on a meaningful measurement scale.
- **Trends** are the rate of performance improvement or continuation of good performance in important areas over time.
- **Comparisons** include your performance relative to that of other appropriate organizations.
- **Integration** is the degree to which your performance measures address important performance requirements related to customers, products, markets, processes, action plans and objectives across the organization, as well as in process elements.

"These categories provide a holistic approach to organizational improvement, and the criteria emphasize continuous improvement, innovation and results-oriented performance."[2]

The book "A new Capstone - Decision making with discernment" shows how to build discernment, following these guidelines.

The Baldrige Excellence Framework has a global reputation

The book "A new Capstone - Decision making with discernment" will rely on the Baldrige because of its undisputed global prestige.

ChatGPT shows us why the Baldrige Excellence Framework enjoys a worldwide reputation due to several key factors:

1. Comprehensive and rigorous standards. The framework provides a robust set of criteria that organizations in different sectors can adopt.
2. Success and proven results. The framework has a track record of helping organizations improve their performance.
3. Continuous improvement and innovation. The Baldrige framework emphasizes a culture of continuous improvement, innovation and learning.
4. Global applicability. Although it originated in the United States, the framework is universally applicable.
5. International recognition and adaptations. Many countries have adapted the Baldrige Framework to create their own national models of excellence. For example, Japan has the Deming Award, and Europe has the European Foundation for Quality Management Excellence Model.

---

[2] Ibid.

6. Focus on leadership and strategy. The Baldrige framework places a strong emphasis on leadership, vision and strategy.

7. Trusted by governments and organizations around the world. The framework is endorsed by the U.S. government (through the National Institute of Standards and Technology) and is supported by many international organizations.

8. Holistic approach to performance excellence. The framework focuses not only on financial performance, but on the overall health of the organization, including customers, employees and the community, through sustainable and responsible business practices.

9. Collaboration with other frameworks. The Framework often works in tandem with other international quality and management systems, such as ISO standards or Lean and Six Sigma.

10. Educational and development support. The Framework offers extensive educational resources, workshops and training to help organizations improve.

11. Focus on results. The Framework emphasizes results-oriented performance.

12. Based on core values and concepts. The Framework is based on core values that align with universal business principles such as customer focus, integrity, innovation and social responsibility.

13. Supporting organizational alignment. Emphasizes the need for organizational alignment, which means ensuring that an organization's strategy, processes and people work together toward a common purpose.

14. Holistic quality management system. The Framework provides a holistic quality management system that integrates various management disciplines, such as strategic planning, performance measurement and operations improvement, into a unified system.

15. Encourages employee engagement and development. The Framework places significant emphasis on workforce engagement and development, recognizing that employees are critical to the success of any organization.
16. Adaptable to any stage of organizational maturity. The Framework is scalable and can be applied to organizations at various stages of maturity.
17. Global thought leadership. The Program has contributed to global thought leadership in the field of organizational excellence, in academic literature, business journals and international forums.
18. Facilitates continuous learning. Promotes a culture of learning at all levels of an organization, new practices, continuous self-assessment, and knowledge management.
19. Recognition and awards. The Baldrige Award is one of the highest national honors in the United States, and its prestige has made it a worldwide benchmark for best practices, with an international reputation as a symbol of excellence.
20. Promotes sustainability and social responsibility. Promotes sustainable practices, social responsibility and ethics.
21. Promotes adaptability and resilience. The framework emphasizes adaptability to change and the ability to respond effectively to external challenges, to build resilience by incorporating flexibility and responsiveness.
22. Increased global collaboration and networking. Promotes global collaboration through its network of award winners, evaluation experts and organizations. Encourages the exchange of best practices, fostering a community of like-minded organizations committed to excellence.

23. Support for long-term competitiveness. Helps organizations achieve a sustainable competitive advantage, with a long-term perspective, regardless of market fluctuations.

24. Global training and consulting support. There is an extensive network of consultants, educators and trainers around the world who specialize in the Baldrige Excellence Framework.

25. Transparency and objectivity in evaluation. The Baldrige Framework evaluation process is based on objective criteria and rigorous assessment, making it a transparent and fair approach to organizational improvement.

In summary, the Baldrige Excellence Framework is recognized worldwide for its comprehensive, adaptive and results-oriented approach to improving organizational performance. Its commitment to continuous improvement, leadership and sustainability aligns with the needs and challenges of companies around the world. It fosters a culture of excellence that resonates around the world, making it relevant across industries and countries. By offering a structured yet flexible model that can be applied across industries and cultures, it has earned the trust and admiration of organizations worldwide.

Appendix 1

Calculation of economic value creation

The following methodology is used in this book to calculate the three pieces of information that appear in all the strategy-value creation charts.

- **EVA**

For the EVA formula, we use an approximation of the original McKinsey's formula[1]

EVA = (NOPLAT / OC) - (0.042 + Beta * 0.038)

NOPLAT = Normalized Income - Interest Income + Interest Expense, provided by Yahoo Finance, in the Financials sheet, Income Statement, for the last 5 years.

OC = Total Assets - (Cash, Cash Equivalents & Short Term Investments) - (Payables And Accrued Expenses), provided by Yahoo Finance, in the Financials, Income Statement, for the last 4 years.

Beta provided by Yahoo Finance, in the Summary sheet.

For example, for United States Steel Corporation (X) the url is:

https://finance.yahoo.com/quote/X/

---

[1] Copeland, Tom, et al. *Valuation: Measuring and Managing the Value of Companies.* 3rd edition. McKinsey & Company Inc. John Wiley & Sons, Inc. 2000.

The EVA model [EVA = net operating profit after tax - (invested capital x weighted average cost of capital)] leads to exactly the same value as the DCF [PV = CF1 / (1+r) + CF2 / (1+r)2 + … [T / (k - r)] / (1+r)n-1, which means: PV = present value; CFi = cash flow in year I; n = number of periods; r = discount rate; T = cash flow in the terminal year; g = expected growth rate].

- **Sales Growth**

To calculate the Sales Growth, we used the Revenues data for the last 10 years provided by ROIC.ai

For example, for United States Steel Corporation (X) the url is:

https://www.roic.ai/quote/X/financials

- **Intellectual Capital**

To calculate the Intellectual Capital we used the P/B of the last 5 years provided by Mornigstar.

For example, for United States Steel Corporation (X) the url is:

https://www.morningstar.com/stocks/xnys/x/valuation

- **Classification of companies into business segments**

The classification of companies into business segments is based on the website

For example, for United States Steel Corporation (X) the url is:

https://www.roic.ai/quote/X/financials

Appendix 2

Analysis of the Competitive Environment. Critical Thinking.

To determine competitive strategies, the competitive environment must first be analyzed, identifying which of the four types of competitive environments the business segment is operating in: perfect competition, monopolistic competition, oligopoly, and monopoly.

This exercise is crucial because it helps determine the type of competition in the business segment (or company), and this is the first step in defining the competitive strategy and exploring the possibilities of achieving positive economic benefits.

The following analysis is based on the intuitions of Microeconomics, Managerial Economics, and Industrial Economics.

Perfect competition versus monopolistic competition.

A first set of factors analyzes whether competition is perfect or monopolistic. It is essentially an extension of Michael Porter's factors, as explained in his book Competitive Strategy, with the addition of some new factors contributed by Industrial Economics (IE).

The factors that indicate an environment of perfect competition or monopolistic competition are:

- A larger number of competitors reduces the MP (market power).
- The existence of fixed costs (e.g., new investments, branding, advertising, promotions) increases the level of competition and reduces MP.

- Horizontal differentiation (e.g., geographic differentiation, tastes, ages, fashions, socioeconomic differences) increases customer transportation costs and reinforces MP.
- The existence of multiple options and the availability of products that reduce transportation costs and foster perfect competition (reduces MP).
- Vertical differentiation (e.g., quality, durability and reliability as sources of MPcreation).
- Strategic impact (e.g., certain products or businesses that are critical to a company's future cash flow and must be defended, even with short-term losses).
- Exit barriers (e.g., the cost of exiting a business is evaluated in a company's strategic decisions, accepting a low price as a better alternative to leaving the business).
- Existence of substitutes that reduce market power according to Lerner.
- Customer-related factors that reduce market power. Firms concentrate sales to a single powerful customer, or a single customer buys most of the firms' turnover; purchases account for a significant portion of a customer's costs; products are standard or undifferentiated; customers can switch suppliers at very low cost; customers earn low profits; customers pose high backward integration risks; products are not important to the quality of customers' products; customers have complete information, demand, market prices, costs, etc.

Oligopoly

The second set of factors examines when competition is oligopolistic. Both EI (collusion) and FVR factors (the relationship with competitors and the ability to learn and harmonize with them are considered key resources) are taken into account. The literature is extensive in this area; this chapter reflects concepts from Chamberlin[1], Rotemberg and Saloner[2], Tirole[3], Shy[4], Basu[5], Besanko[6], Wilson[7], Dixit and Nalebuff[8], Dixit and Skeath[9], Pindyck and Rubinfeld[10] and Martin[11].

The IE factors that indicate an oligopolistic market are:

- The maturity of the market (companies have been in business for many years) increases the capacity for collusion and MP.

---

[1] Chamberlin, E. Duopoly. Value where sellers are few. Quarterly Journal of Economics. 1929.

Chamberlin, E. The theory of monopolistic competition. Cambridge. Harvard University Press. 1933.

[2] Rotemberg, J and Saloner, G. A supergame-theoretic model of business cycles and price wars during booms. American Economic Review. 1986.

[3] Tirole, Jean. The theory of Industrial Organization. The MIT Press. 1998

[4] Shy, Oz. Industrial Organization. The MIT Press. 1995

[5] Basu, Kaushik. Lectures in Industrial Organization Theory. Blackwell Publishers. 1993

[6] Besanko, David; Dranove, David; Shanley, Mark. Economics of Strategy. Wiley. 2000

[7] Wilson, Robert. Non-linear pricing. Oxford University Press. 1993

[8] Dixit, Avinash K. Nalebuff, Barry J. Thinking Strategically: The Competitive Edge in Business, Politics, and Everyday Life. W. W. Norton & Company. 1993

[9] Dixit, A. Skeath, S. 1999 Games of Strategy. Norton and Co. New York.

[10] Pindyck, Robert; Rubinfeld, Daniel. Microeconomics. Prentice Hall. 1995

[11] Martin, Stephen. Advanced Industrial Economics. Blackwell. 1999

- Market atomization reduces MP, as small competitors do not collude because they can make large sales gains by reducing prices, with a low risk that larger competitors will react.

- Lack of information on competitors' movements and poor interaction complicate collusion and reduce MP.

- Fluctuating demand, especially high levels of sales growth, makes collusion unlikely, as potential colluders' profits from cheating are high, reducing MP.

- The different financial situation of the players complicates collusion and reduces MP; distressed competitors do not collude because they have high financial costs and risk bankruptcy; consequently, they prefer short-term gains and are willing to default on collusion.

- The different cost structure of the players reduces the ability to collude and reduces PM; competitors with a low-cost structure prefer competition by reducing prices, obtaining additional economies of scale and eliminating competitors.

Monopoly

The third set of factors examines the case of perfect monopolies, where there is no competition. The criteria of the Stackelberg-Spence-Dixit model, as presented by Tirole (1998), are followed. The Stackelberg-Spence-Dixit model presents the IE view of high barriers to entry through the concept of capital and overlaps with the unique resources concept of FVR.

- Experience, technology, and high innovation capacity are key resources that raise barriers to entry and deter potential new entrants.

- Strong customer relationships are a key resource, leaving no residual demand for future new entrants through promotions, consumer loyalty programs, miles, long-term agreements, cross-selling, and combo offers, as well as CRM strategies, thereby deterring new entrants.
- Businesses that require economies of scale as key resources, as new entrants may not be willing to incur losses until they reach a certain level of economies of scale and prefer to stay out of the business.
- Control of channels as a key resource (e.g., exclusive franchise network) that complicates the entry of new players.
- Strong horizontal differentiation can become a key resource, as it can increase customer carrying costs, switching costs, and require more effort from potential participants.
- A low-cost structure is a key resource that deters potential new entrants.
- Government policies, such as regulations to defend a monopoly or patent, may inhibit the entry of new entrants.

Appendix 3

Analysis of Strategies. Critical Thinking.

Competitive and marketing strategies. Critical thinking.

To create economic value, companies must have a positive Economic Value Added (EVA), based on their competitive environments or strategies. Figure 27. shows how the EVA model allows framing the correlation between competitive environments, competitive strategies, and economic benefits.

Competitive environment

Competitive strategies

Financial results

Correlation: environment, strategies, results

| Perfect Competition | Monopolistic Competition | Oligopoly | Monopoly |

Growth

| Correlation: environment, strategies, results | Correlation: environment, strategies, results | Correlation: environment, strategies, results | Correlation: environment, strategies, results |

Perfect Competition

1. Cost efficiency, lean manufacturing, economies of scale
2. Reduction of competition: consolidation
3. Promotion strategies: imperfect information
4. Distribution strategies: push strategy, low level channel, logistics

Monopolistic Competition

1. Product strategies: differentiation and positioning, innovation. Strong branding and packaging
2. Pricing strategies: linear and non-linear, bundling and tying (promos, combos, long term agreements)
3. Promotion strategies: pull, advertising and personal selling. Customer relationship
4. Distribution strategies: push / channels, logistics, supply chain management

Oligopoly

Collusion on specific variables of the marketing mix (avoid competing in prices, differentiation, innovation, etc.)

Monopoly

1. Experience, technology, innovation, capital
2. Switching costs: CRM
3. Increase scale economies predatory price
4. Block distribution channels
5. Predatory Differentiation, advertising
6. Government policy.

STRATEGIES BASED ON ACTIONS

STRATEGIES BASED ON RESOURCES

-2%   0%   6%   10%

Economic Profits - EVA

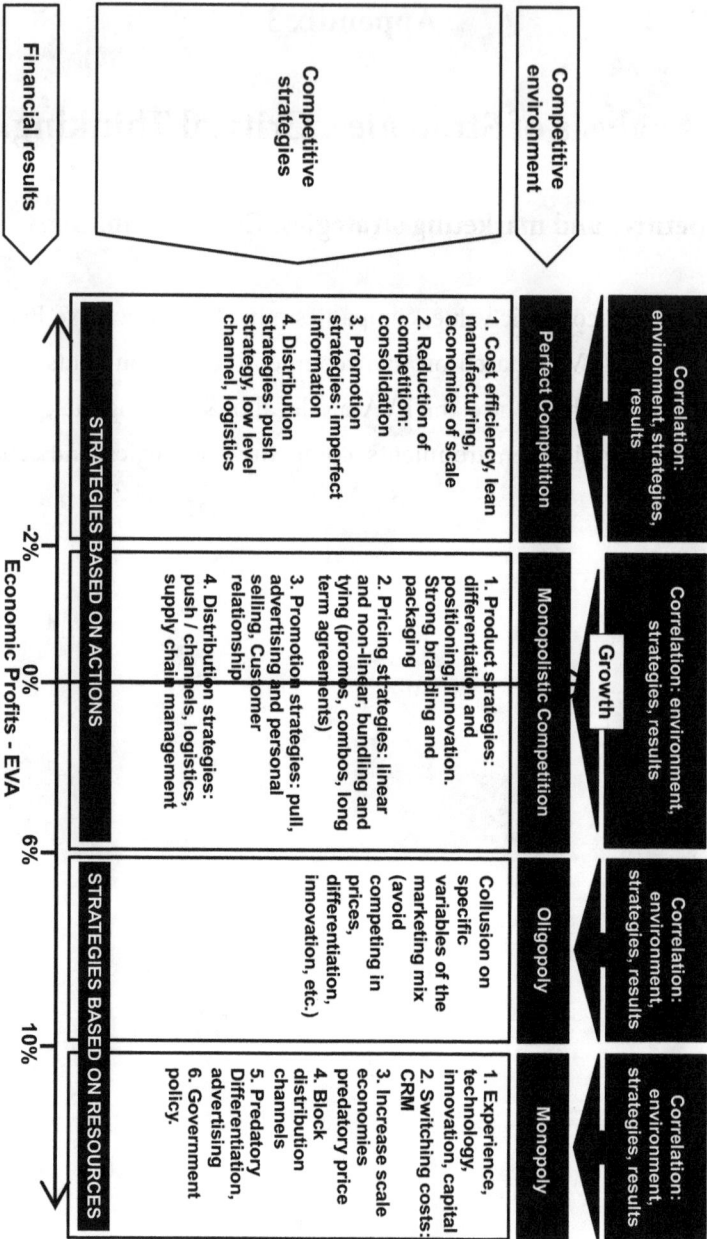

Figure 27. Correlation between competitive environment, competitive strategies, and economic performance (EVA).

According to the EVA model, to create economic value, an economic agent needs to have positive economic benefits (EVA); it must have a profitability above the average of similar organizations, which generates the need for successful competitive strategies.

The "Economic Benefits (EVA)" metric is crucial. Traditional accounting measures an organization's accounting profits, also referred to as accounting results, as its revenues minus its costs.

The EVA[1] measures the economic benefits, comparing the profitability of the company to that of similar companies. For example, if my company's profitability is 15% and the profitability of the competition is 10%, my company has an EVA of 5% (15% - 10%), i.e., it creates economic value. This means that the capital I invest in new resources enhances the value of my company.

But if the profitability of my company is 10% and that of the competition is 15%, the EVA of my company will be -5% (10% - 15%), destroying economic value. This means that the more I invest, the less my company will be worth.

This is crucial in the world of strategic management because it is not enough for an investment to be profitable; for an investment to be appropriate, it must be more profitable than an investment in an alternative business. EVA is based on a comparison: to be successful, we have to be better than others.

---

[1] Economic benefits = Capital invested * (Return on invested capital - Opportunity cost of capital).

Perfect competition. Environments, strategies, and results. Critical thinking.

Michael Porter, in his famous book "Competitive Strategies" defined two competitive environments, perfect competition and monopolistic competition, and two groups of strategies, low cost and high differentiation.

Firms operating in competitive environments of perfect competition (on the left of Figure 27) tend to have very low economic profits (EVA less than -2%).

Competitive strategies are summarized as:

- **Cost efficiency.** Since in perfect competition companies cannot determine prices (the markets determine them) and products cannot be differentiated, the main competitive strategies are aimed at keeping costs low by increasing efficiency, through Lean Manufacturing or by trying to increase sales volumes to generate economies of scale that reduce unit costs. Consolidation through mergers, acquisitions, and alliances helps to generate these economies of scale and also reduces the intensity of competition. However, this strategy is not always possible. Acquisitions can be difficult because players may not have the financial resources to acquire their competitors. Alliances between competitors do not always work.

- **Pricing**. Since the market defines the price, they cannot have pricing strategies.

- **Products**. Products are usually standard and cannot be differentiated. Product strategies tend toward standardization and simplification to minimize costs.

- **Promotion**. Promotional strategies may not be advisable: the more information available, the more perfect the competition becomes, and the more power is given to the customer to select the competitor with the lowest price. Additionally, a company's promotional efforts may inadvertently benefit the competition.

- **Distribution**. Distribution strategies are limited to the push strategy (selling through channels) with a low-level, frugal channel, combined with low-cost logistics, which aims to simplify distribution and reduce costs.

Typical industries that usually operate in perfect competition are raw materials, agribusiness, natural resources, metals, and chemicals, among others.

Natural resources and metals have low market power and negative EVA, because of the inability to differentiate. Although they are mature businesses, it is unlikely that competitors will be able to collude, given the high atomization of these businesses.

Chemicals have a similar situation; however, in some specific cases, a smaller number of competitors may allow for some degree of collusion.

Airlines have a negative EVA, as they can hardly differentiate themselves. However, in some cases, based on unique resources (e.g., Southwest Airlines) or increased consolidation and regulatory protection in the industry, they may be able to improve their EVAs.

Dotcoms are in a very difficult situation. Perfect information makes the competition perfect; it is easy for customers to get all the information on competitors' products and choose the cheapest one. In addition, it is easy for service providers to imitate what competitors do. The low transportation cost of customers (an industrial economics concept that reflects the ease with which customers can switch from one supplier to another) leads to perfect competition, as suppliers cannot differentiate themselves. In some cases, dotcoms may not operate in perfect competition, as transportation costs (Porter called them switching costs) may be high in some cases, as once customers become familiar with one service provider (Amazon, Google, eBay), it may be challenging to switch to another, giving them some degree of market power.

Monopolistic competition. Environments, strategies, and results. Critical thinking.

Firms operating in monopolistic competition (in the center of Figure 27) have EVAs close to zero.

The products can be differentiated, but differentiation is based on actions that competitors can imitate, not on unique resources that competitors cannot imitate. In the long run, investment efforts are not always recovered due to the rapid competitive reaction.

Competitive strategies are based on high differentiation, which are the ones recommended by most marketing management textbooks:

- **Product strategies** are based on differentiation and positioning, with a focus on brand and packaging.
- **Pricing strategies** enable a range of linear and non-linear pricing options, including promotions, combos, and long-term agreements.
- **Promotional strategies** are related to pull strategies, such as advertising, personal selling, and customer relationship management.
- **Distribution strategies** can be based on more sophisticated push strategies, such as utilizing higher-level channels with added value (e.g., insurance, consulting, financing), as well as advanced logistics and supply chain management.

Typical industries that tend to operate in monopolistic competition are: mass consumption, food, automobiles, and electronics.

Mass-consumption products may have temporarily positive EVAs, based on some degree of differentiation, brand-based protection, or switching costs. In some cases, they may have good EVA based on some collusion as a result of market maturity.

Automakers can become differentiated, but intense competition from cost-efficient manufacturers and advancements in technology in Asian countries make collusion impossible, leading some of them to low EVAs.

Basic telephony struggles with commodity syndrome. In some cases, government protection allows a local telephone company to be profitable. In residential telephony, location is another factor that enables some companies to have a degree of market power. Unfortunately, long-distance telephony does not enjoy these advantages and, consequently, has negative EVAs.

Pricing strategies

The classical supply and demand curves in monopolies provide a framework for analyzing this phenomenon. If a firm determines a single price for all its customers by following the prices of its competitors, the price will be the "price in perfect competition". However, some customers are willing to pay a higher price, so the firm does not make a corresponding profit.

The way to maximize profits is to charge each customer a different price; this is called price discrimination and has a huge impact on strategic management, as it gives rise to two very common promotional tools: promotions and combos.

In promotions (EI calls it "bundling"), sales units are based on the same product; for example, customers may pay $5 for a half-foot sandwich, but for $6 they get a one-foot sandwich.

In combos (EI calls it "tying"), sales units incorporate other products. For example, McDonald's may offer a Big Mac for $2, a Coke for $2 and a serving of fries for $2, but all three together cost $3.

Non-linear pricing essentially means selling more volume by reducing prices.

Wilson[2] explains how nonlinear pricing offers customers a menu of choices tailored to their preferences, allowing for discrimination and leveraging the firm's market power.

If the firm has competition and tries to charge a price above the perfect competition price, customers will not buy from it. If the firm tries to charge a price lower than the perfect competition price, it may trigger a price war; all competitors will reduce their prices, and the firm will make even less profit.

Wilson demonstrates that in many businesses, such as railroads, cell phone services, water, and others, the application of non-linear pricing results in a variable unit price. The unit price depends on the quantity of service provided. It is based on discounts applied by the company, which in turn are based on sales volume, contract duration, use of a consumer card, mileage, etc. Rail rates are based on weight, volume, and distance; electric rates are based on consumption and time of day; airlines with frequent flyer discounts are based on mileage, advance purchase, and round trips; equipment rental is based on length of contract; advertising is based on space, location, and time.

Wilson explains a popular application of nonlinear pricing: two-part tariffs. He presents several examples of ways to price discriminate using two-part tariffs, which involve a fixed fee and a variable fee linked to the amount of consumption. For example, these include initial gym payments

---

[2] Wilson, Robert. Non-linear pricing. Oxford University Press. 1993

and monthly fees, telephone services, gas and electricity (with monthly fees based on consumption), cab initial payments, and distance-based fees.

Wilson's mathematical models demonstrate that price discrimination can be exercised in the fixed portion of the tariff, and that this portion generates the majority of profitability.

Horizontal differentiation

The fundamental strategy in monopolistic competition is differentiation, which can be categorized into two types.

Horizontal differentiation refers to attributes that are appreciated differently by different customers. Some people prefer dark chocolate over milk chocolate, while others love cinnamon rolls, and some may not. Additionally, gas stations and banks are often located in specific areas that may be convenient for some customers but inconvenient for others.

The key issue is: the greater the differentiation, the better for some customers and the worse for others. Therefore, differentiation attracts some customers but drives others away.

In such cases, how can it be determined whether differentiation is beneficial?

Jean Tirole (Nobel Prize 2014) in his famous book "The Theory of Industrial Organization", incorporates a model called "linear city"[3] to analyze this dilemma.

---

[3] According to Tirole (1998): The utility "U" for a customer decreases if the price "p" he pays y increases with his transportation cost t, and the distance between what he wants (x) and the product position (a).

$U_x = -p_A - t(x - a)$ if he buys a product located in A
$U_x = -p_B - t(x - (L - b))$ if he buys a product located in B

The linear city can be visualized as a beach where two Coca-Cola sellers are located at different points, and a potential customer is situated somewhere in between. The seller must decide the best price for the Coke.

Where will the customer buy? It depends on prices, but also on the distance the customer must travel. For example, if one seller sells Coke for $2 and the other for $1, but the latter is a kilometer farther away, our customer will most likely pay the $2 for a Coke and buy from the closer seller.

The linear city model introduces a new concept: **the consumer's transportation cost**. This refers to the effort a consumer makes to adapt to a product, including its features, location, flavors, and so on. For example, the transportation cost is the emotional cost that a 15-year-old girl will pay to wear a cheap dress to the prom, and this is a cost that must be added to the actual price of the dress.

Tirole shows that profitability should be zero if the customer is exactly in the middle between the two products and there is no differentiation. The profits of both firms are zero, which means perfect competition.

But there is another interesting conclusion from the mathematical model: the higher the customer's transportation cost, the greater the possibility of differentiation, and therefore, the greater the profitability of each company. If the customer must walk a kilometer to buy a cheaper Coca-Cola, he will most likely accept paying a higher price to buy the one that is closer. Higher transportation costs allow for greater differentiation. The task of a company's manager is to determine transportation costs, which means identifying the attributes that are important to customers. Otherwise, products become undifferentiated, and competition becomes perfect.

It is possible to calculate the demand of each company and, therefore, its profits. The profitability will be::

$$\pi^A = t * (3L - b + a)^2 / 18$$

This concept is fundamental in the new economy, the world of the Internet, because the cost of transporting the customer can be negligible (just one click). In contrast, in the real world, it can mean several kilometers, a lot of gasoline, and considerable time to go from one supplier to another. Many companies that enthusiastically entered the web to sell their products ignored the fact that they were creating an environment of perfect competition by eliminating the cost of transportation.

Tirole states that whenever a company differentiates itself from others, two effects occur.

The demand effect requires that, to gain market share, both companies must be close to customers. The problem is this: the demand effect acts like a magnet, attracting all sellers to the exact locations, which eliminates their differentiation. This drives businesses to be similar, unintentionally pushing them toward standardization. Tirole mentions bookstores near a university, fishermen in a harbor, stores in shopping malls, and websites on the Internet. In these cases, competition should be perfect, and their profitability very low.

Tirole describes a second effect: the strategy effect, which means that by increasing differentiation, companies can raise their prices, even if this forces them to avoid popular areas, thus reducing sales volume. It is like selling a bottle of water in the middle of the desert: the price will be very high, but demand will be very low.

Vertical differentiation

In vertical differentiation, all consumers agree that the more differentiated a product is, the higher their satisfaction. Typical attributes that every customer wants include quality, reliability, durability, and other similar characteristics.

According to Tirole, the important aspect of vertical differentiation is the fact that, if two competitors have the same degree of vertical differentiation, their profitability will be zero, since they do not differentiate, and this leads to perfect competition.

Quality in some industries is a requirement to stay in the market, but not necessarily a source of lasting competitive advantage. Quality may not provide real competitive protection.

Oligopolies. Environments, strategies, and results. Critical thinking.

Companies operating as oligopolies tend to have higher economic profits, with EVA often exceeding 10%.

The core of an oligopoly strategy is that firms do not compete in some aspects of the marketing mix, typically price.

Figure 27 shows that strategies in perfect and monopolistic competition are action-based, while strategies in oligopolies and monopolies are resource-based. The key resource of oligopolies is maturity; competitors have learned to avoid competing on price.

Some industries operate as oligopolies, including glues, corn flakes, peanut butter, mobile telephony, petroleum, and certain branded products.

Coca-Cola and Pepsi, the cola producers, are protected by their high differentiation (brand) and, consequently, can behave as an oligopoly, avoiding price competition.

Cell phone companies used to behave like perfect competition during their early years, as high growth prevented them from colluding because they needed to increase their customer bases. However, today, that growth is slower, allowing them to ease competition based on market maturity.

Oil is a commodity and, consequently, should have a negative EVA. However, production is concentrated in a few countries, working as a cartel. This collusive behavior allows oil to enjoy a very good EVA. However, due to international politics, the cartel does not always work so well, and some years, it fails, generating low EVA.

Oligopolistic competition strategies

For Tirole, collusion strategies should be understood as a game where several players participate; each has rewards (gains) and punishments (losses) for its strategic actions. These rewards and punishments lead companies to modify their behavior to learn. Companies must learn and mature, in the same way that animals are trained based on rewards and punishments, and children are educated and mature. And the result of that maturation is learning a lesson: "The less we compete, the better". Competition produces price wars and losses (punishments), while non-competition produces good profits (rewards).

The key issue is that companies can learn how to behave in the competitive game to increase their rewards, i.e., their profits.

Tirole introduces a conceptual model that helps understand the factors that influence a collusive strategy: the supergame[4]. The model is based on

---

[4] The model shows what happens after several periods. The vertical arrows represent the revenues of each company.

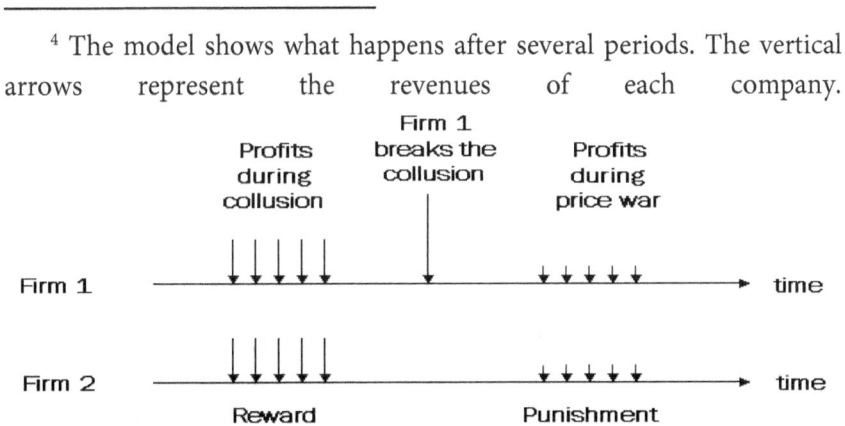

	Firm 1	
Profits during collusion	breaks the collusion	Profits during price war

Firm 1 ———————————————————→ time

Firm 2 ———————————————————→ time

Reward   Punishment

two competitors who have previously established a collusive strategy. Collusion means that both will keep prices high.

The profit level is higher when both competitors behave as an oligopoly; when they keep prices high, both companies are highly profitable.

However, firm 1 decides to reduce prices without telling firm 2 to increase its market share.

Initially, this benefits company 1 by increasing its market share. But company 2 realizes what has happened and decides to react by reducing its prices; the collusion breaks down, and a price war breaks out.

Who wins? The answer is nobody. The price war is negative for both competitors. Their market shares do not change, and their revenues are reduced. It is a punishment.

What can happen next? It is very likely that both competitors will realize that cheating is not a good idea. Maintaining collusion is the best way to obtain higher profits.

If this is correct, why is collusion not very common? If it is just a matter of learning how to collude, why is collusion not much more common?

The answer is that players may have different motivations, strategies, and drives.

- **Market atomization**

A collusive strategy does not work when the market is atomized, as small players can break the collusion because they get potentially very high rewards (increased market share) but no punishments (no price war). Any of the small players can end up getting a large reward by lowering prices and gaining a larger market share. Since the market is atomized, if a small competitor increases its market share, the impact on the competitors' market may be negligible. When a small competitor decides to reduce its prices, the large competitors may not notice the insignificant loss of market share and, consequently, may not react; the small competitor may grow without any retaliation from the large competitors. A small competitor may not appear to be a real threat to the large ones.

- **Different cost structures**

According to Tirole's supergame, if two competitors have different cost structures, the one with the lower costs will be tempted to compete with low prices. Different cost structures make collusion unfeasible.

- **Unstable demand**

Collusion is impossible to maintain if demand is growing rapidly or when there is uncertainty about future demand. According to Tirole, it is easy to implement a collusion strategy when demand is stable. There is no gain for an opportunistic competitor, as retaliation can be immediate and a price war will ensue. However, when demand fluctuates during periods of high demand growth, the opportunistic competitor is motivated to lower prices and gain market share. As demand grows, the rewards for lowering prices and gaining market share can be very large. The punishment for breaking collusion is insignificant relative to the rewards.

- **Different financial situations of the stakeholders**

A collusive strategy is not viable if competitors have different financial situations, since the less financially secure players will be more opportunistic and will break the collusion. Firms in a precarious financial situation have a higher cost of funds, so they prioritize the short term. These firms tend to be more opportunistic and more likely to play their own game and cheat in collusions. These companies ultimately need to break the law to survive. It is a well-documented fact that corruption and deal-breaking are more prevalent in vulnerable environments, as people and companies become more opportunistic and focused on the short term because they need to survive in the present. Collusion is not viable with them.

Conversely, well-established companies with a sound and stable financial situation have a lower cost of funds, will defend collusive strategies and high prices, and will not engage in unnecessary and destructive short-term price wars.

- **Competitor maturity**

Maturity facilitates collusion. Tirole's supergame leads to another very important concept: firms with seniority, well-established cash flow and low financing cost, which have been in the market for many years, are likely to have suffered price wars wrongly triggered to gain market share; that market share did not materialize and it took them a long time to recover the price. This repeated punishment taught them that price wars are undesirable and that collusion is a better strategy for everyone. These companies became prudent and mature. Mature companies try to avoid war on price, differentiation, advertising, etc.

- **Infrequent interaction or limited information**

Collusion is not feasible when companies do not have good information on their competitors' movements. According to Tirole, it is difficult for colluders to act in a coordinated manner if they do not know what the other is doing. For collusion to be efficient, it is important that one competitor knows what the other is doing and can react quickly to punish the partner if the partner cheats.

- **Limited horizon**

Another interesting idea of Tirole's supergame is that if the future is near, there is an incentive to break the collusion since the punishment may have no effect. This is the case of employees who announce that they are going to resign from the company. After that, they can break all the rules; there is no punishment.

Monopolies. Environments, strategies, and results. Critical thinking.

Companies that operate as pure or near-pure monopolies have the highest economic profits.

Monopolistic strategies are related to the accumulation of unique and inimitable resources, or, in other words, capital. Strategies depend on the existence of potential new entrants, who may lead the incumbent firm to accumulate more capital to prevent their entry, collude with them, abandon perfect monopoly, and move to oligopolistic strategies.

Stackelberg's model[5] shows how, to be profitable, a company needs to have more capital (unique resources) than the competition: if a company

---

[5] $d\pi^2/dK_1 = /\ K\partial\pi^2\partial_1 + /\ x\partial\pi^2\partial_1 dx_1^{\cdot}/dK_1 + /\ x\partial\pi^2\partial_2 dx_2^{\cdot}/dK_1$

$d\pi^2/dK_1 =$ the total effect of K_1 on π^2 is the sum of the following three terms.

$\partial\pi^2/\ K\partial_1 =$ the direct effect of firm 1's investment K on firm 2's performance: If K_1 is the cumulative customer base before the entry of firm 2, the more customers, the smaller the size of the market remaining for firm 2, and π^2 shrinks.

$\partial\pi^2/\ x\partial_1 dx_{(1)} (\cdot)/dK_1 =$ the strategic effect (next period): K_1 forces a change in the ex-post behavior x of firm 1, thus affecting the future of firm 2 and, consequently, forcing firm 2 to take actions that resist the actions of firm 1.

has little capital, that gives it little market power, innovation may be too risky and inadvisable: the financial efforts associated with innovation may not be recouped, as a competitor may reach the market earlier. If profits are low, growing may increase losses. This implies that innovation is rather improbable in environments of intense competition. As Schumpeter stated, innovation makes sense in monopolistic situations and helps to preserve and defend the monopolistic situation.

IE suggests that monopolies have maintained high EVA because they have high barriers to entry that prevent potential competitors from entering the business. The resource view of the firm (RVF), on the other hand, explains that unique and hard-to-imitate resources provide firms with stable cash flow. Monopolistic strategies are based on unique and inimitable resources. The more capital they have managed to develop in unique resources, the higher the barriers to entry.

The word "resources" here has a broader meaning: expertise, technology, innovation, capital, customer or channel relationships, customer switching costs, economies of scale or scope, channel control, strong image, government policy such as patents or market protection (utilities), and others.

In some cases, new competitors are inevitable, and in such cases, it is better for a monopolist to soften competition and adopt an oligopolistic strategy of "friendly collusion."

$(x / \partial_1 \dot{} \partial_1) K =$ which affects the profits of company 2 in proportion to $(/ x \partial \pi^2 \partial_1)$.

If $d\pi^2/dK_1 < 0$, the investment places firm 1 in a hard position; if, on the contrary, $d\pi^2/dK_1 > 0$, firm 1's position is soft. To prevent the entry of firm 2, firm 1 will be hard and overinvest.

Typical monopolists are: Microsoft (Windows and Office), some utilities with market protection, some pharmaceutical companies (in patent-protected products), and others.

Microsoft, specifically in products such as Windows or Office, enjoys an almost perfect monopoly situation with extraordinary EVAs (its market share is close to 100%). Both products became the standards and, consequently, any computer user needs them to interact with other users. In addition, the huge investments Microsoft made to improve these products prevent potential competitors from entering the business. In other segments, however, Microsoft is not a monopolist.

Kirin (beer, Japan) enjoyed market share levels of 80% in the past. Very high fixed costs (advertising and distribution) generate high economies of scale, which puts small competitors in a weak position and makes it impossible for them to compete. A company with a 5 percent market share cannot afford to have a national distribution system or a national advertising campaign versus Kirin with its 80 percent share.

The factors that facilitate a monopoly are:

- **Experience, technology, innovation, capital**

Microsoft (in Windows and Office products) is the perfect example; in addition to the standard it has created, which makes it impossible for Windows and Office users to abandon those products, it is impossible for a potential competitor to invest the billions of dollars invested by Microsoft or match Microsoft's experience.

- **Switching costs**

They represent the effort that the customer must make to change suppliers. For example, if you want to change your bank, you must unsubscribe from all the services and utilities that have direct debits on your account, which takes time. Customer relationship management (CRM) is a strategy for building stronger relationships with your customers; for example, Amazon uses market information and knowledge of your past purchases to offer you books you might like.

- **Increased economies of scale**

Like the Kirin brewery in Japan, which has an 80% market share and can absorb fixed costs, such as advertising and distribution, much better than its competitors.

- **Low prices**

Like Wal-Mart, which eliminated its competitors in small towns using its cost efficiency and economies of scale.

- **Blocking of distribution channels**

Such as Japanese producers who do not allow foreign companies to use established channels.

- **Predatory differentiation**

Advertising such as that used by cola producers.

- **Government policy**

Such as some regulated utilities or pharmaceutical companies with patent protection.

Unique and inimitable barriers to entry and resources

Two different economic theories explain the higher profits.

- Industrial Economics: industries obtain high profits when entry barriers are high.
- The Resource View of the Firm: profits are the result of unique, inimitable, and scarce resources.

Entry barriers	Unique, inimitable, scarce resources
Experience, technology, innovation	Organizational resources, knowledge, routines, processes, dynamic capabilities
Capital requirements	Physical and financial resources
Exchange costs, customer relationship	Relations
Economies of scale, predatory pricing and price discrimination	
Blocking distribution channels	Licenses, relationships
Differentiation, publicity, image, public approval	Ability to satisfy stakeholders, ability to communicate, communication skills
Government policy	Patents

Figure 29. Market power integrates industrial economics and the resource view of the firm.

Figure 29 shows how critical thinking in strategic management integrates both: high barriers to entry or uniqueness of resources produce market power, responsible for high profits.

This shows that both economic benefits (EVA) and intellectual capital (MVA) are fundamental to understanding whether an organization can create economic value.

Many excellent and modern companies invest money in physical assets, which have a market value similar to or lower than that of their physical assets. They cannot create intellectual capital or unique resources to support their strategies.

According to IE, when entry barriers are low, in perfect or monopolistic competition, markets and market power are low, competition is intense, and profits are low or zero.

According to the RVF, in perfect or monopolistic competition, firms cannot have unique and inimitable resources, since they rely on easily imitable actions or imitable physical resources. In oligopolistic markets with greater market power, what EI calls collusion is equivalent to RVF's ability to operate in harmony with competition. In fully monopolistic markets, what EI calls barriers to entry is equivalent to RVF's unique resources.

Growth and innovation strategies. Critical thinking.

To create economic value, companies need sales growth based on their innovation strategies (new products, customers, markets, businesses, channels).

Figure 30 shows how innovation strategies can create or destroy economic value.

Economic results

Environment and innovation strategies

Innovation strategies based on RESOURCES (RVF and IE)

Innovation through McKinsey's capability platform:

1. Business-specific core competences.

2. Growth-enabling competences (financing, risk management, deal structuring, regulatory management, capital productivity enhancement)

3. Privileged assets (brands, network, intellectual property, infrastructure, information, licenses).

4. Special relationships (access corveying, capability complementing).

Innovation strategies based on ACTIONS

1. Innovation through acquisitions, alliances, or internal development (new customer segments, new products, new geographies, new businesses, new value composition of the value chain, and increase in customer share).

2. Predatory Marketing. Price Discrimination.

Growth

Economic Profits - EVA

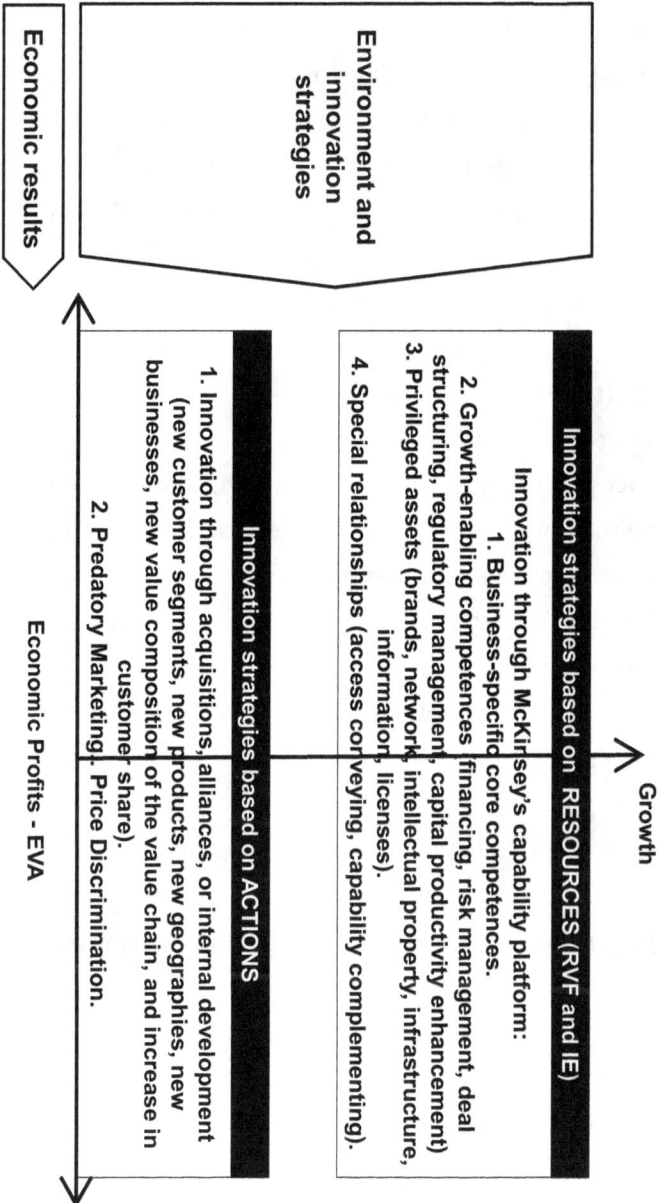

Figure 30. Correlation between innovation strategies and sales growth.

Innovation requires unique and inimitable resources to be sustainable. McKinsey's Baghai, Coley, and White[6] made an outstanding contribution in this area, "Staircases to Growth". McKinsey states that in order to have a successful innovative strategy, companies must have the following set of resources, or as McKinsey calls it, Capability Platform: Business Specific Core Competencies, Growth Enabling Competencies (acquisitions, financing, risk management and deal structuring, regulatory management, capital productivity enhancement), Privileged Assets (brands, networks, intellectual property, infrastructure, information, licensing), Special Relationships (access, complementing capabilities).

The lower part of Figure 30 shows that companies can grow based on actions, and that these actions will produce a low level of growth because they are easily imitable by the competition, or on unique and inimitable resources to maintain high levels of growth that the competition cannot imitate, as McKinsey proposes.

McKinsey proposes a cautious way of managing innovation strategies based on a progressive learning process.

- Horizon 3: Create viable options. Companies should start by developing options, creating new medium-term alternatives that provide the company with new options for future growth. Options are small steps, small investments in new ventures, pilot experiments, and field studies. If an option, an experiment, is successful, the company can move on to the next horizon.
- Horizon 2: Create emerging businesses. The successful business option in Horizon 3 has been moved to Horizon 2, and successful businesses can move to the first horizon.

---

[6] Baghai, M. Coley, S. White, D.. Staircases to Growth. McKinsey and Company. 1996

- Horizon 1: Expand and defend the core business. The business has now succeeded and has become a full-fledged start-up. The growth strategy has proven its effectiveness, and the company can now fully invest in it.

McKinsey describes seven steps to growth: 1. Increase in customer share, 2. Increase in market share, 3. Innovation in products and services. 4. Acquisitions, 5. Innovation in the value chain, 6. New businesses, 7. New markets: geographical expansion.

Several authors have demonstrated the limitations of innovation strategies in terms of their ability to create stock market value.

Stephen Martin presents a model to describe innovation[7], linking environment, strategies and results, promoting critical thinking; according to the model, innovation only works if the innovating firm has market power.

---

[7] $E = (n - 1) V [r + (n - 2) h]/(r + nh)3 + \{2V [(r + (n - 1) h]/(r + nh)3 + dF2 /dh2 \} > 0$

V will be the profit obtained by the first company to patent its invention.

i is the company committed to R&D.

h_i is the intensity of i's effort in R&D.

t_i is the random time it may take to complete the i project, distributed according to: $1 - e^{-hit}$

$E(t_i)$ is the expected time to complete the project = $1/h._i$

$F(h)$ is the initial investment at the start of a project.

The expected profits for the company will be: $E(p_1) = h_1 V/(r + h_1 + h_2) - F(h)._1$

r is the discount rate, when the future values of the profits v are subtracted.

n is the number of competing companies.

Companies often invest money in a new company, without considering whether it will have enough demand if the competition is developing a similar or better product or service. There are a lot of companies that make huge investments to grow and these investments do not have enough market power. As a result, EVAs are negative and the initial investment is never recovered.

Resource strategies. Critical thinking.

The market value of a company is equal to the initial capital invested, its physical capital, plus the economic value that the company is capable of generating over its lifetime, its Market Value Added[8] (MVA). According to the EVA model, the MVA = present value of future EVAs. The MVA reflects the future, what investors are willing to pay for the company over and above its book value, based on the expectation that the company can generate positive economic returns and growth in the future. That future is based on its resources and intellectual capital, which are measured by the difference between the organization's market value and its physical capital in terms of book value.

Modern economics, strategic management, and international business assert that success is based on resources. The view of the firm as a pool of resources (RVF) asserts that unique and inimitable resources are at the heart of business success.

---

[8] McKinsey formulates the MVA with the following equation, which provides very interesting data: (Economic profit T+1 / WACC) + NOPLAT T+1 * (Growth g / ROIC) * (ROIC - WACC) / [WACC * (WACC - Growth g)].

Kaplan and Norton[9] classify intangible resources into: human (employee skills, talent, and knowledge); information (databases, information systems, networks, and technology infrastructure); and organization (culture, leadership, employee alignment, teamwork, and knowledge management).

Leif Edvinsson summarizes an organization's resources in **intellectual capital**: **human capital** (knowledge), **social capital** (relationships), **renewal capital** (innovation), and **process capital** (equipment and technology).

---

[9] Kaplan, R. Norton, D. The Balanced Scorecard. Harvard Business School Publishing. 1996

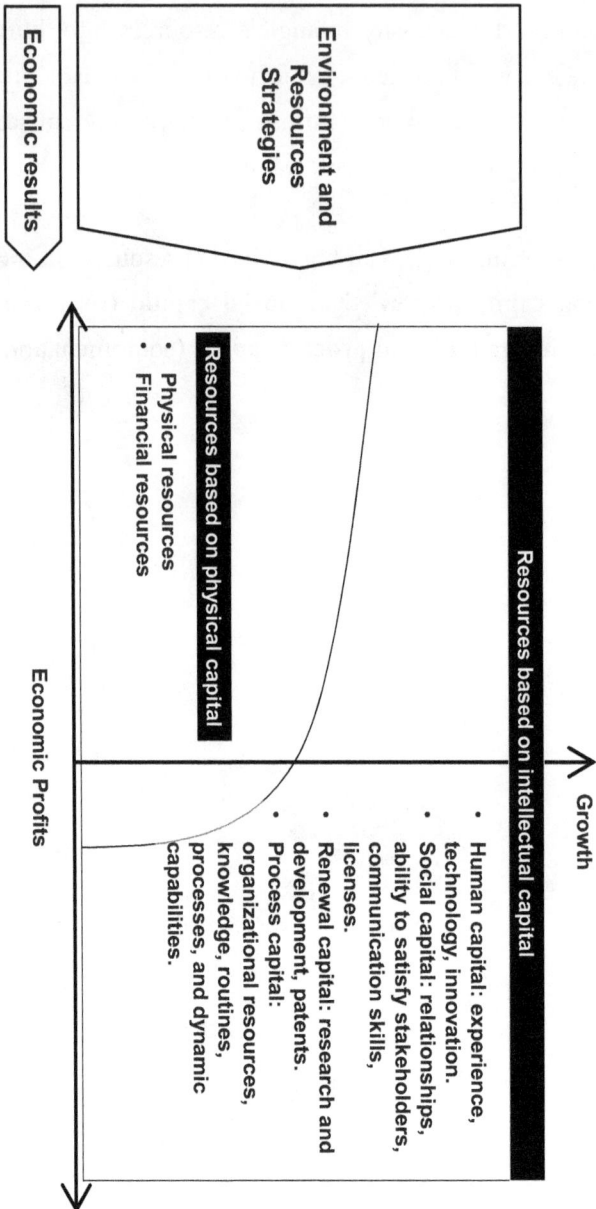

Figure 31. Correlation between resource strategies, EVA and sales growth.

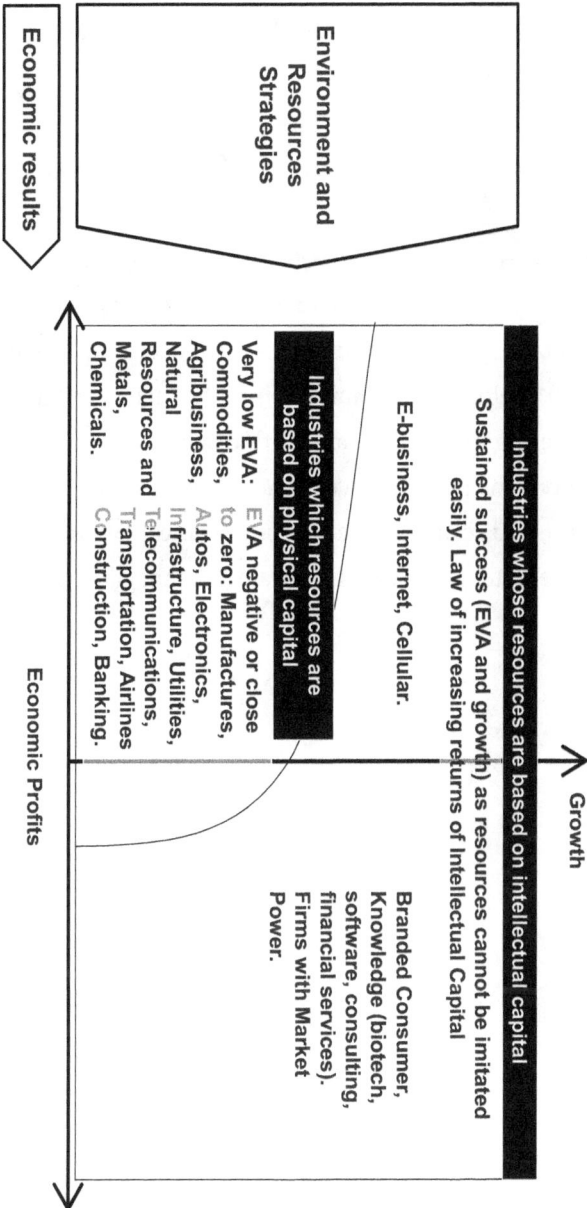

Figure 32. Economic value creation and resources, by industry.

How should these resources be coordinated, whether in-house, shared, or outsourced, and how should they be structured?

Corporate resources and strategies. Critical thinking.

For Porter[10], a pioneer in this debate, the most important contribution of corporate strategy to a company's success is defending synergies; synergies help maximize the use of corporate resources, creating cost efficiencies (a profit driver), helping companies reinforce their strengths (a profit driver), and fostering innovation (a growth driver).

The EVA model helps analyze corporate strategies in terms of environments, strategies, and results. It is a source of critical and interdisciplinary thinking and integrates and simplifies strategic management.

---

[10] Porter, M. Competitive advantage. The Free Press. 1985.
Porter, M. Competitive strategy. The Free Press. 1980.

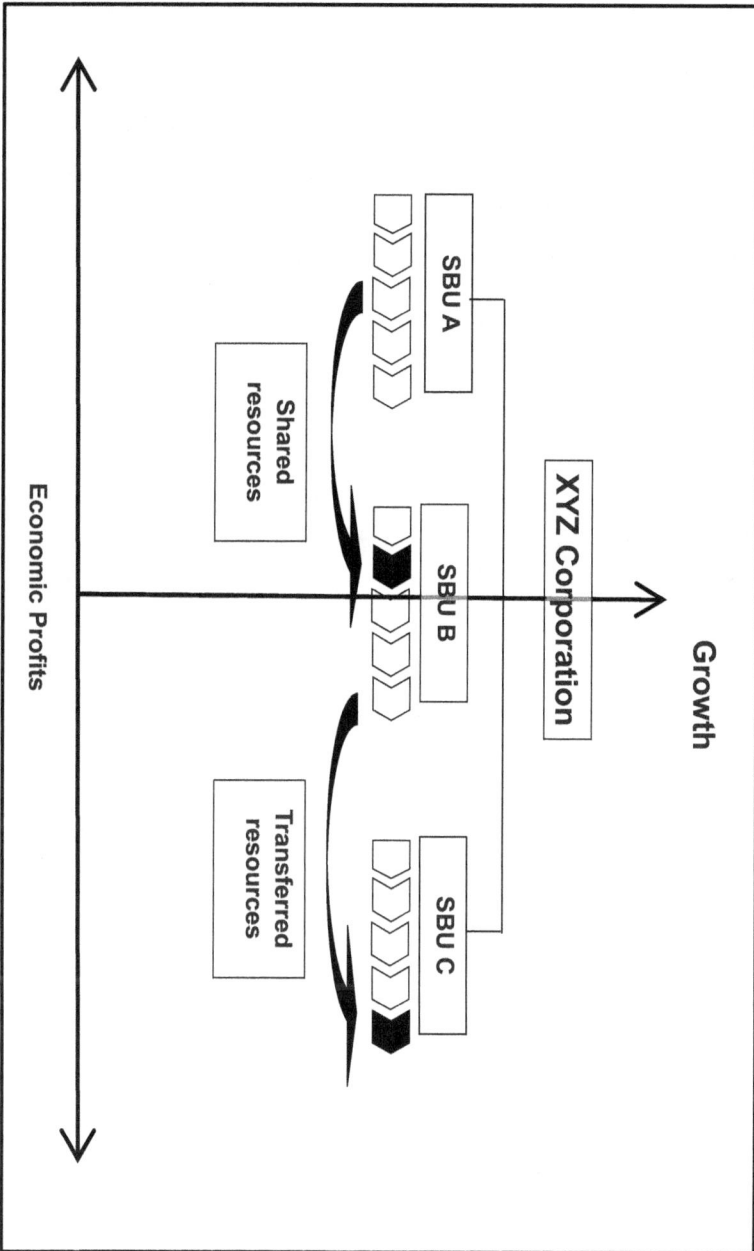

Figure 33. Corporate strategies and economic value creation.

According to Michael Porter's seminal research,[11] "From Competitive Advantage to Corporate Strategy", the benefits of having corporations with several strategic business units (SBUs in the chart) should be based on the impact of resources, aligning corporate strategy with resource strategies. According to Porter, a corporate strategy can generate synergies by sharing or transferring resources between business units.

Strategic alliances. Critical thinking.

Reve[12] has a very powerful framework that extends Porter's five forces and incorporates the resources of alliance partners into each force to analyze the benefits and problems of strategic alliances.

Reve shows how strategic alliances are a privileged way to expand the use of resources by sharing them with other companies, which helps produce economies of scale (profit drivers), economies of scope (growth drivers by strengthening innovation) and economies of integration (profit drivers by strengthening market power).

---

[11] Porter, Michael E. "From Competitive Advantage to Corporate Strategy" in *Harvard Business Review* 65, 3 (1987), https://hbr.org/1987/05/from-competitive-advantage-to-corporate-strategy.

[12] Reve, T. The Firm as a Nexus of Internal and External Contracts. Sage Publications. 1990. The article is reproduced at: De Wit, Bob. Meyer, Ron. Strategy; process, content, context. West Publishing Company. 2004.

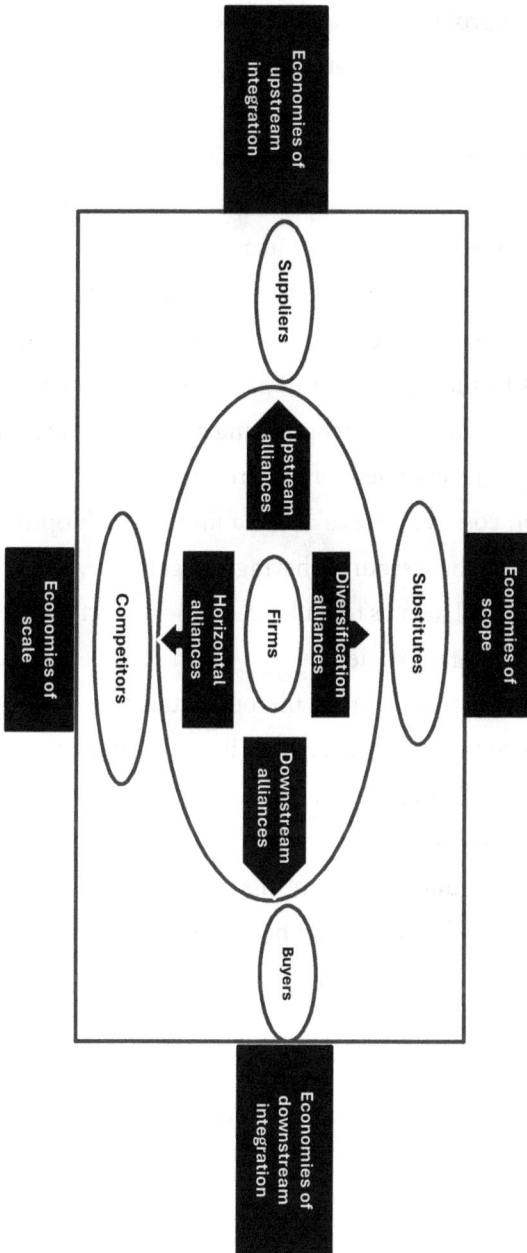

Diversification alliances provide economies of scope (sharing resources for different goods and services: Microsoft uses programmers to develop different products, or Amazon uses its channels to sell many products). These types of alliances are useful to grow in new areas through diversification.

Horizontal alliances provide economies of scale. This type of alliance facilitates the exchange and control of competitive resources and is useful for avoiding competitive wars, thus increasing profits.

Upstream and downstream alliances provide economies of integration. They help share resources (e.g., superior logistics and marketing). This integration leads to the creation of market power through lower costs and higher quality, as well as the strengthening of relationships with buyers and suppliers and the development of joint resources.

Transaction cost economics[13] puts a limit to such optimism, showing the risks and costs that resource sharing can generate. The combination of both approaches will help us to understand the impact of this aspect on the creation of stock market value.

Transaction costs arise from the opportunistic behavior of partners. For example: a company discovers that its main supplier is unreliable and this affects its own production; a contractor receives an advance payment and then goes bankrupt.

Contracts can limit these problems, but contracts may be incomplete, and opportunistic behavior cannot be completely eliminated (bounded rationality, difficulties in specifying or measuring performance, and asymmetric information).

Functional strategies. Critical thinking.

---

[13] Williamson, Oliver E. Economics and organization: A primer. California Management Review. Berkeley. 1996.

The three strategies we have seen, competitive, innovation, and resource strategies, are an organization's general strategies, and they predetermine its functional strategies.

Marketing strategies. Critical thinking.

We have already seen how marketing strategies are strongly linked to competitive strategies.

As shown in Figure 27, perfect competition and monopolistic competition strategies are the backbone of the Marketing Mix: price, product, promotion, and placement (distribution).

Operations strategies. Critical thinking.

Operations strategies depend on the competitive environment, and competitive, innovation, and resource strategies.

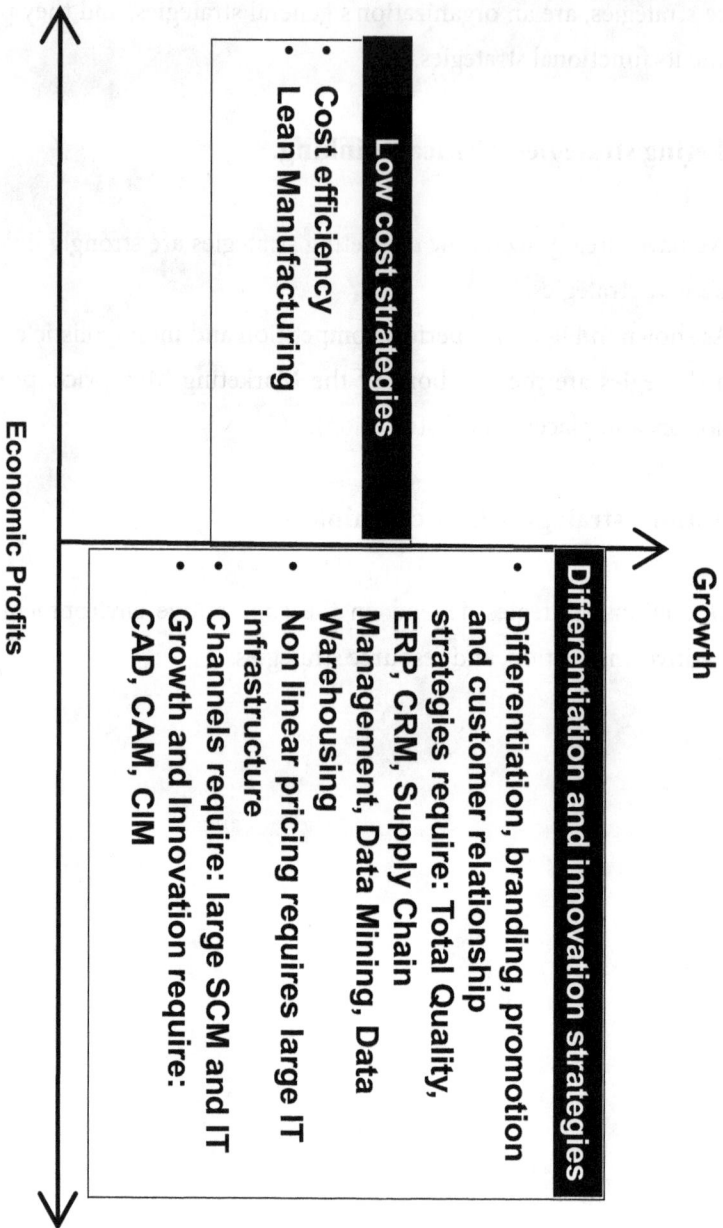

Figure 34. Operations strategies and economic value creation.

On the left side of Figure 34, in the negative economic benefits quadrant, when low cost and efficiency are the main competitive strategies, the organization should focus on cost efficiency and lean manufacturing as operational strategies.

On the right side of Figure 34, in the positive economic benefits quadrant, the organization must be integrated into the environment when differentiation and innovation are the main competitive strategies. In other words, it needs to know the needs of its customers, what the competition is doing, and what technology providers can do to make strategic decisions. This requires some specific operational strategies, such as total quality management (to orient internal processes towards the customer) or information technology resources such as enterprise resource planning (ERP to organize information efficiently), customer relationship management (CRM to keep track of customer relationships), supply chain management (SCM to manage the supply process), data mining and warehousing (to identify business issues that may affect the customer).

Organizational strategies. Critical thinking.

Organizational strategies depend on the strategic environment, and competitive, innovation, and resource strategies.

Figure 35 frames the four organizational models proposed by Gareth Morgan[14] in *Images of Organization.*

---

[14] Morgan, Gareth. *Images of Organization.* SAGE Publications. 2006.

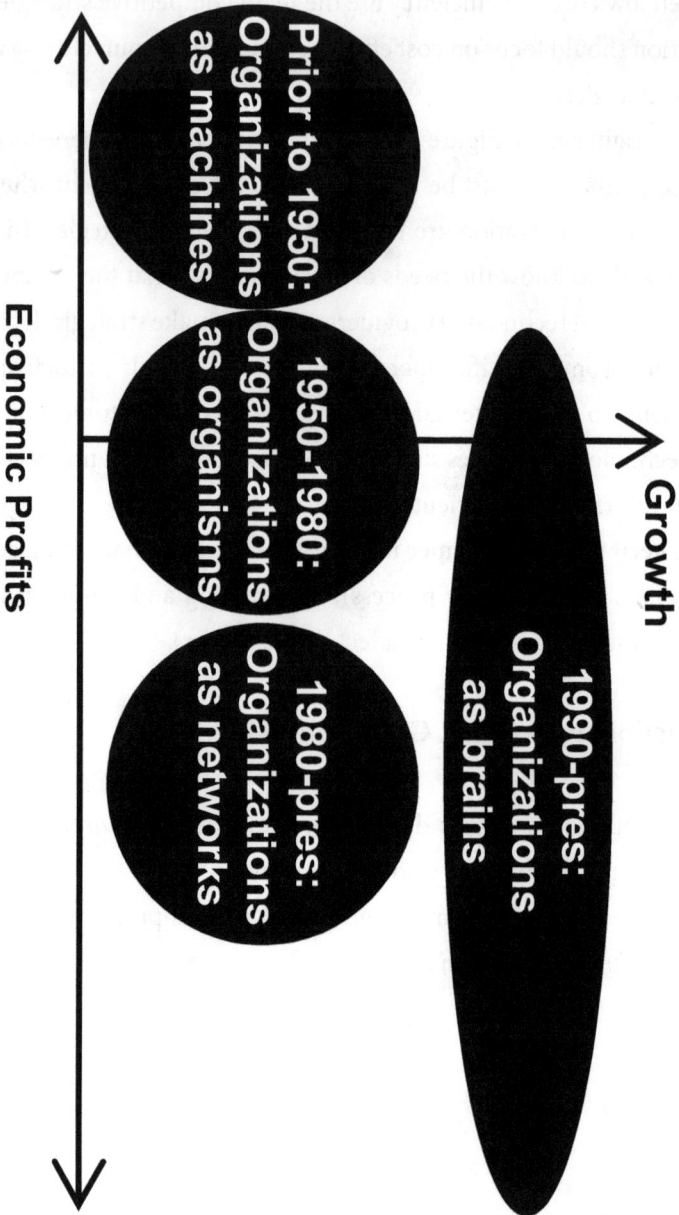

Figure 35. Organizational strategies and economic value creation.

On the left side of Figure 35, with negative economic benefits, are machine-like organizations in a perfectly competitive environment with low-cost strategies.

In the center of Figure 35, organizations as organisms are suitable for monopolistic competition strategies, which require a strong market orientation and, consequently, the organization's ability to connect with the environment, to know, feel, and experience what stakeholders feel; this generates differentiation and, consequently, a better economic benefit.

Organizations as networks are appropriate in oligopolistic environments, where organizations follow collusive strategies based on knowledge of competitors' actions and generate positive economic benefits.

Finally, organizations like brains are suitable in monopolistic environments, with high innovation and possibly high market power, leading to sales growth and very positive economic benefits.

On this basis, it is possible to define what type of organizational structure is advisable.

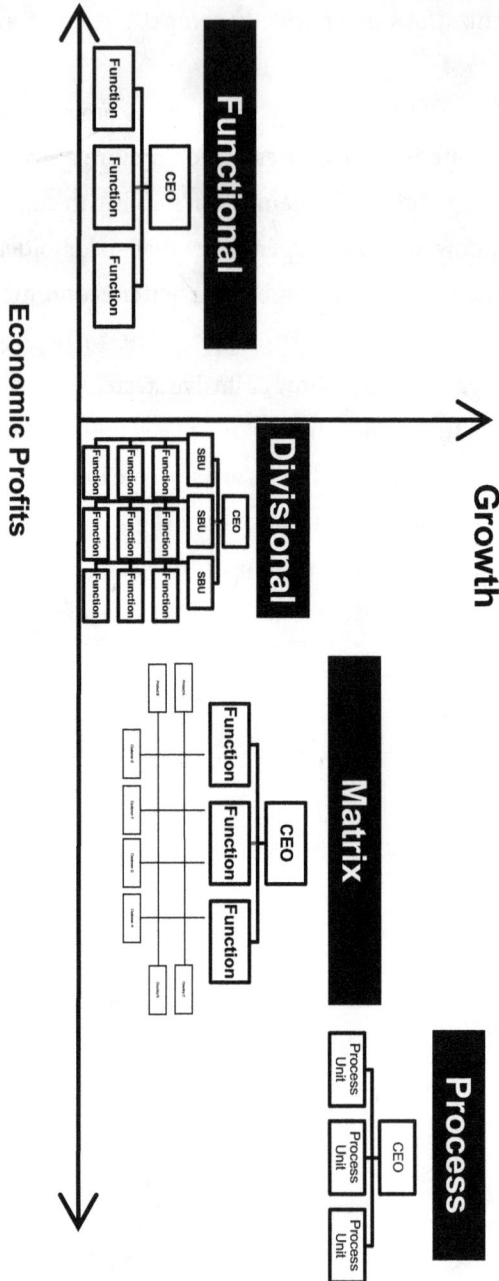

Figure 36. Organizational structures and economic value creation.

On the left side of Figure 36, organizations are more mechanistic. The functional structure is recommended, designed for efficiency, and desirable for organizations operating in stable and predictable environments, such as railroads, raw materials, and water supply. This structure works well in perfectly competitive environments that require efficiency, predictability, and low costs.

On the right side of Figure 36, organizations are more organic, and divisional, matrix, and process structures are recommended. This is because, when the strategic environment is more competitive, growing, innovative, dynamic, and sophisticated, and experiences frequent product changes, the organization must be more proactive, creative, flexible, intelligent, and innovative.

Divisional structures by customer, location, and product are quite organic organizations capable of listening, seeing, and perceiving how the environment feels and reacting to its needs.

The matrix structure coordinates units within other parts of the company, whether functional, divisional, or process. It is even more organic, adaptable, innovative, intelligent, and flexible, with good communication and creativity.

The process structure is a by-product of the reengineering concept of grouping various functions into a team. This provides a much greater degree of flexibility. Not surprisingly, it is particularly suited to innovation strategies (product development, business development, new markets) and competitive strategies (gaining market power through customer service, technical support, and logistics processes).

In this way, the EVA model helps to link the organization's strategies with the environment, strategies, and results.

International strategies. Critical thinking.

The transnational management model of Bartlett, Ghoshal and Beamish, proposes three aspects of international strategy that we will frame in the EVA Model: Figure 37 shows international strategies, Figure 38 shows international organizations and Figure 39 shows international human resources strategies.

On the left of Figures 37, 38, and 39, global organizations are assimilated to the strategies of perfect competition, low cost, mechanistic organizations, and standardization that we saw above. These organizations need significant centralization and coordination of activities to achieve economies of scale, maintain global efficiency, centralize functions, standardize products, and reduce transportation and communication costs. This coordination is achieved through an overall organizational structure based on a divisional product structure, and an ethnocentric staffing (international subsidiaries are filled with employees from the parent company's home country). In this way, product-related functions such as product development, research and development, and manufacturing remain centralized in one place. Obviously, its economic benefits are low.

In the center of Figures 37, 38, and 39, multinational organizations are assimilated to the highly differentiated monopolistic competitive strategies we saw earlier, organic, environmentally sensitive organizations. These organizations operate in sectors that require a strong presence in each country to adapt strategies and products to cultural and social differences, distribution channels, business practices, and political environments, and a polycentric staffing (host-country nationals are required to manage subsidiaries). For example, in sectors such as apparel, food, and cosmetics, different countries have different tastes; therefore, product offerings must be adapted to these realities. Their economic performance is intermediate.

On the right of Figures 37, 38, and 39, transnational organizations are a hybrid of global and multinational organizations, brain, smart, matrix, or process organizations. They must coordinate their strategy and operations worldwide and adapt them to the countries they operate, with geocentric staffing (the best people for key jobs, regardless of their nationality). Their economic performance is high.

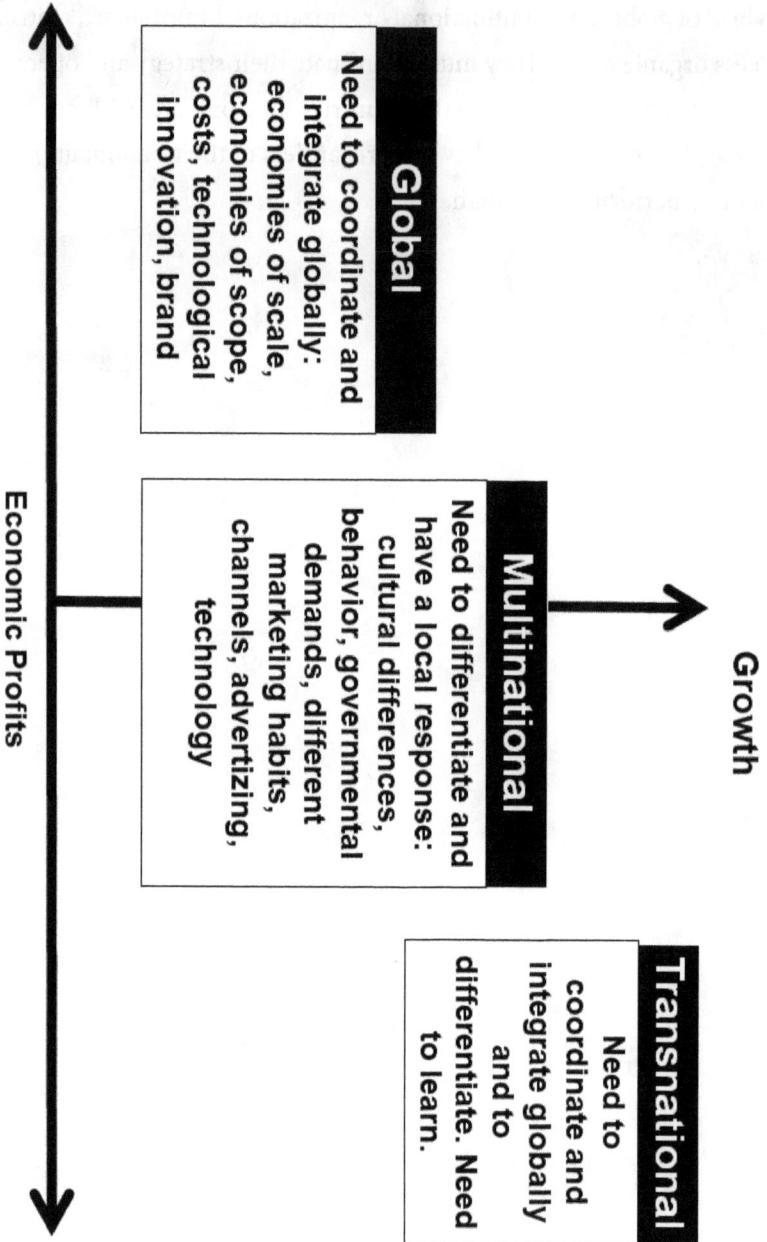

Global

Need to coordinate and integrate globally: economies of scale, economies of scope, costs, technological innovation, brand

Multinational

Need to differentiate and have a local response: cultural differences, behavior, governmental demands, different marketing habits, channels, advertizing, technology

Transnational

Need to coordinate and integrate globally and to differentiate. Need to learn.

Economic Profits

Growth

Figure 37. International strategies and economic value creation.

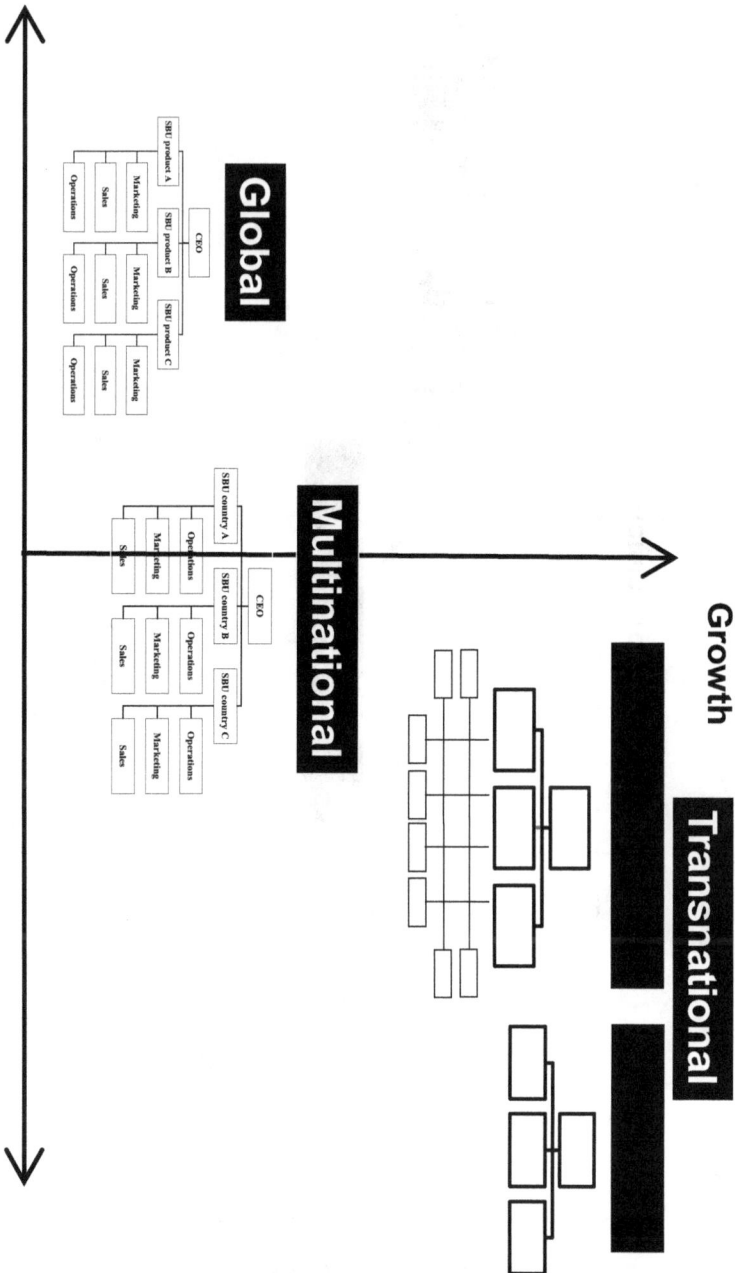

Figure 38. International structures and economic value creation.

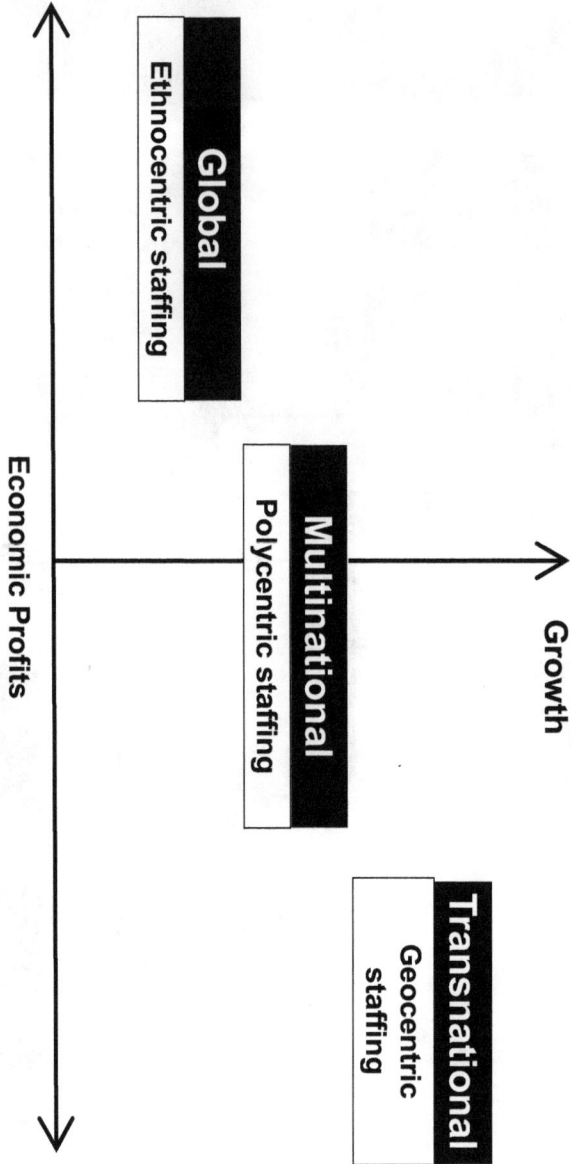

**Figure 39. International human resources strategies
and economic value creation**

Strategic planning. Critical thinking.

The type of strategic planning recommended for each organization depends on the environment, strategies and results.

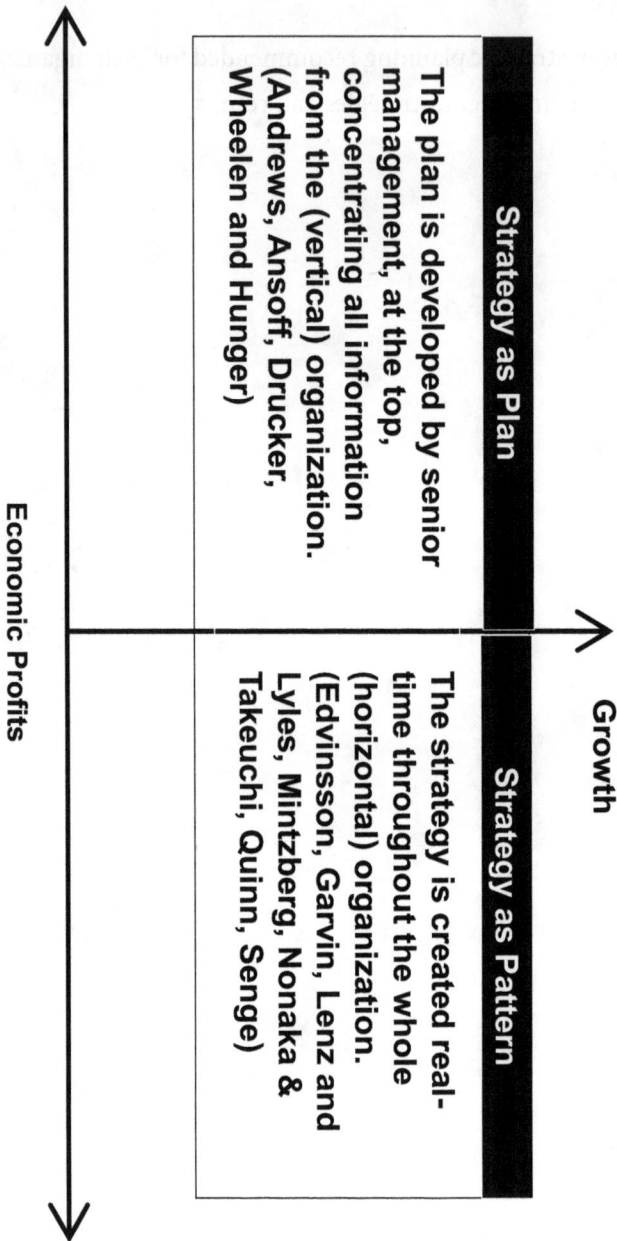

Figure 40. Strategic planning and economic value creation.

On the left side of Figure 40, "strategy as a plan" indicates that the strategic plan is developed at the highest level of the organization. This is typical in mature industries operating in stable and predictable environments where it is difficult to differentiate and innovate, so sophisticated strategic planning is not necessary, and low economic benefits do not allow it.

On the right side of Figure 40, strategy is conceived as a modality, i.e., it emerges from the organization itself. This is typical in environments where companies require high differentiation and innovation, flexibility and agility are crucial, and intellectual capital is vital. In rapidly changing environments, strategic variables are constantly changing, and knowledge and relationships become critical resources needed to ensure a company's success and survival. Strategic planning as a modality refers to the need to use all the knowledge, experience and relationships available throughout the organization, spontaneously generated by employees interacting with customers, suppliers, products and manufacturers, as an organic and cerebral organization.

The business model. Critical thinking.

The modern view of strategic planning emphasizes having the right business model. The business model summarizes how companies make money and involves all business perspectives: customers, employees, processes, innovation, and growth.

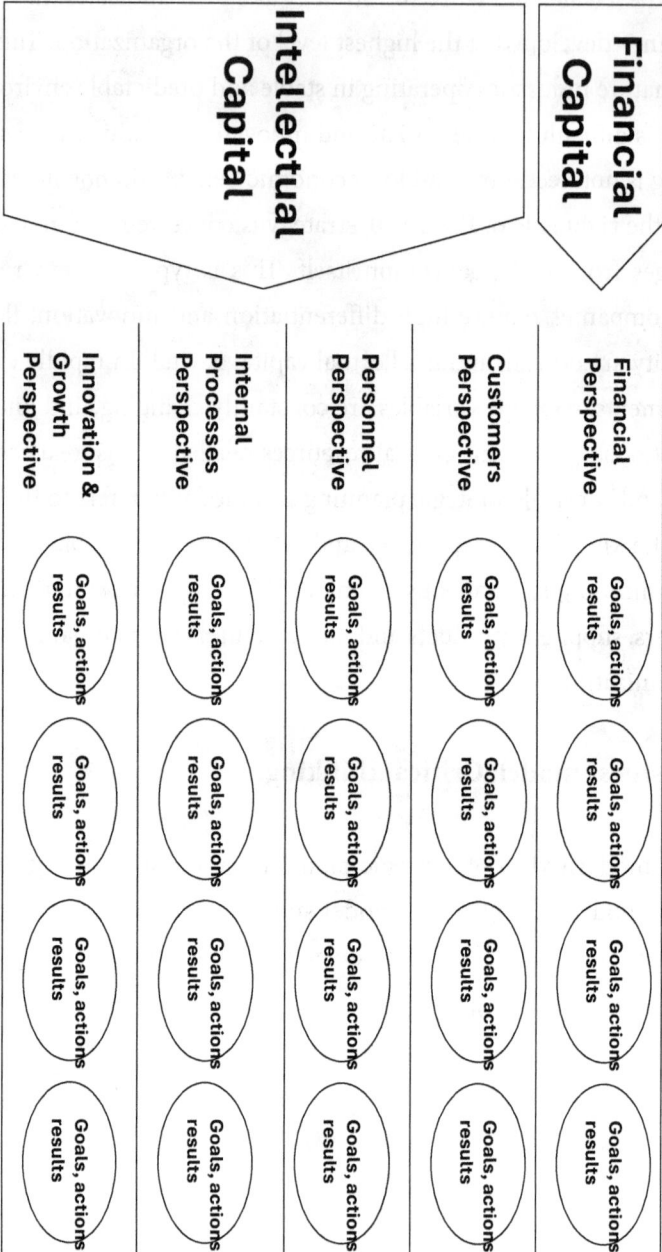

Figure 41. Business model and economic value creation.

The right strategy should be reflected in a business model, a synthesis of how a company can create economic value while satisfying all stakeholders.

Following Leif Edvinsson, there is a profound logic behind the wisdom of the business model: to create economic value, it is necessary to transform intangibles into financial results, so that the economic value of the relationship with customers, employees, suppliers, processes, innovation, etc., can be evaluated.

The business model, also called a Balanced Scorecard, is a mini strategic plan, a synthesis of how to satisfy all stakeholders and which resources to use to create economic value. It helps to analyze, communicate, coordinate, control, and motivate. Today, people use the business model to summarize the plan.

Models and theories of strategic management. Critical thinking.

The EVA model helps to analyze the thinking of many authors, theories, and models of strategic management, which also depend on the environment, strategies, and results. It constitutes a source of critical and interdisciplinary thinking, integrating and simplifying strategic management.

Economic profits

Growth

Low-cost: BCG's learning curve, Porter.

Growth and innovation, McKinsey's 12 ladders, resource-based view of the firm, financial options, industrial economics: Baghai, Coley & White, Chandler, Christensen & Montgomery, Edvinsson, Palepu, Porter, Rumelt, Schumpeter, Wrigley.

Differentiation: Abernathy & Wayne, Andrews, BCG, Kotler, Levitt, McKinsey, PIMS, Porter.

Collusion, Game Theory, Industrial Economics: Bain, Brandenburger & Nalebuff, Chamberlin, Jensen & Meckling, Rotemberg & Saloner, Thompson, Coase, Conner & Williamson.

Monopoly Strategies, Resource-Based View of the Firm, Industrial Economics: Ansoff Barney, Cohen & Levinthal, Cyert & March, Dierikcz & Cool, Edvinsson, Hamel & Prahalad, Hannan & Freeman, Lippman & Rumelt, Mintzberg, Nelson & Winter, Penrose, Peteraf, Pfeffer & Salancik, Prahalad & Hamel, Quinn, Stalk, Teece, Pisano, Shuan, Tushman & Anderson, Wernerfelt.

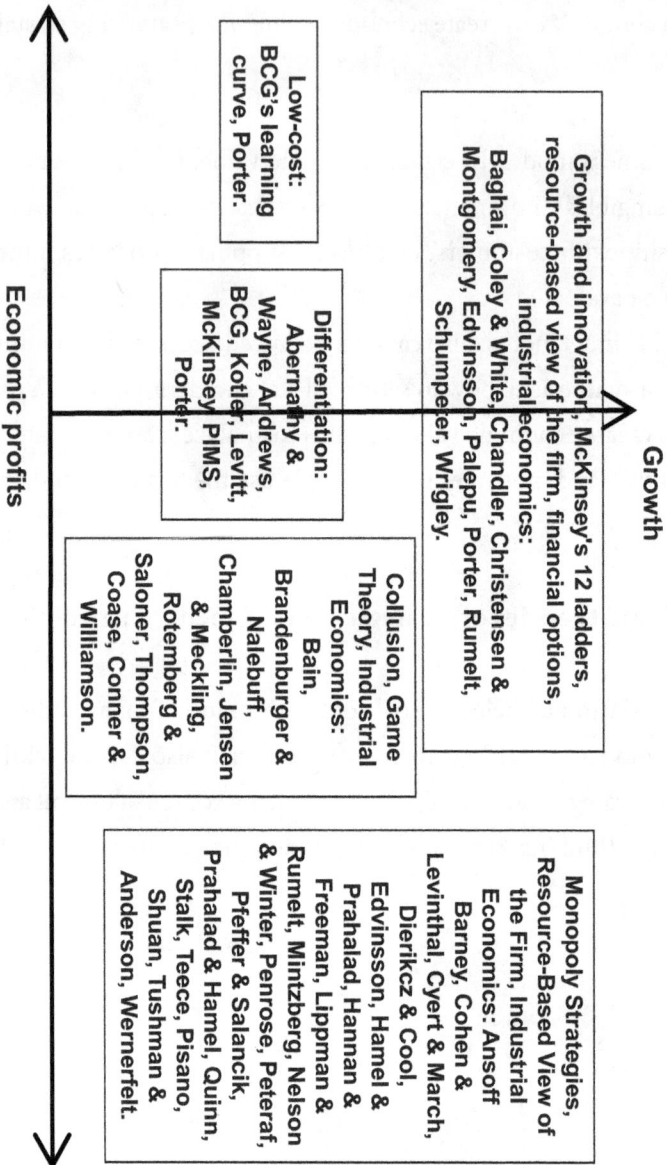

Figure 42. Theories and authors of strategic management and economic value creation.

On the left side of Figure 42, the main theories and models are related to commodity industries, perfect competition environments, low-cost strategies, and negative economic profits. Competition based on cost reduction has led to a perfect competition environment, with products that are *commodities* and low prices, resulting in low economic profits.

In the lower middle part of Figure 42, during the 1960s and 1970s, theories and models prescribe differentiation to reduce competition and increase profitability. The term "differentiation" consolidates a set of theories to produce monopolistic competition. But by the late 1970s it became clear that the strategic actions of monopolistic competition were of limited effectiveness: such strategies are costly to implement and, being based on actions, relatively easy for competitors to imitate. As margins are limited, the economic benefits for these cases are close to 0%.

The theories and models of the next two groups, located on the right of Figure 42, are based on IE and game theory. They rely on non-competition strategies to increase margins, which is common in an oligopoly. Collaboration or developing alliances with competitors softens competition, allowing higher economic benefits.

On the right side of Figure 42, monopoly strategies reflect the theories and models presented by IE, which are based on unique resources.

In Figure 42's vertical dimension, Schumpeter introduced innovation strategies through his "creative destruction" approach. Strategic actions are costly, and competitors can imitate them, destroying economic value. The EVA model shows that innovation strategies succeed based on unique and inimitable resources that generate growth and market power simultaneously.

In this way, the EVA model makes it possible to connect the thinking of many authors working on these issues, the theories and models of strategic management with the environment, with other strategies, and with results.

The SWOT (Strengths, Weaknesses, Opportunities, and Threats). Critical thinking.

- **Strengths and weaknesses. Their linkage with competitive and resource strategies.**

    Determining the strengths and weaknesses proposed by a tool such as SWOT helps to analyze the organization's competitiveness and how strong it is compared to its competitors.

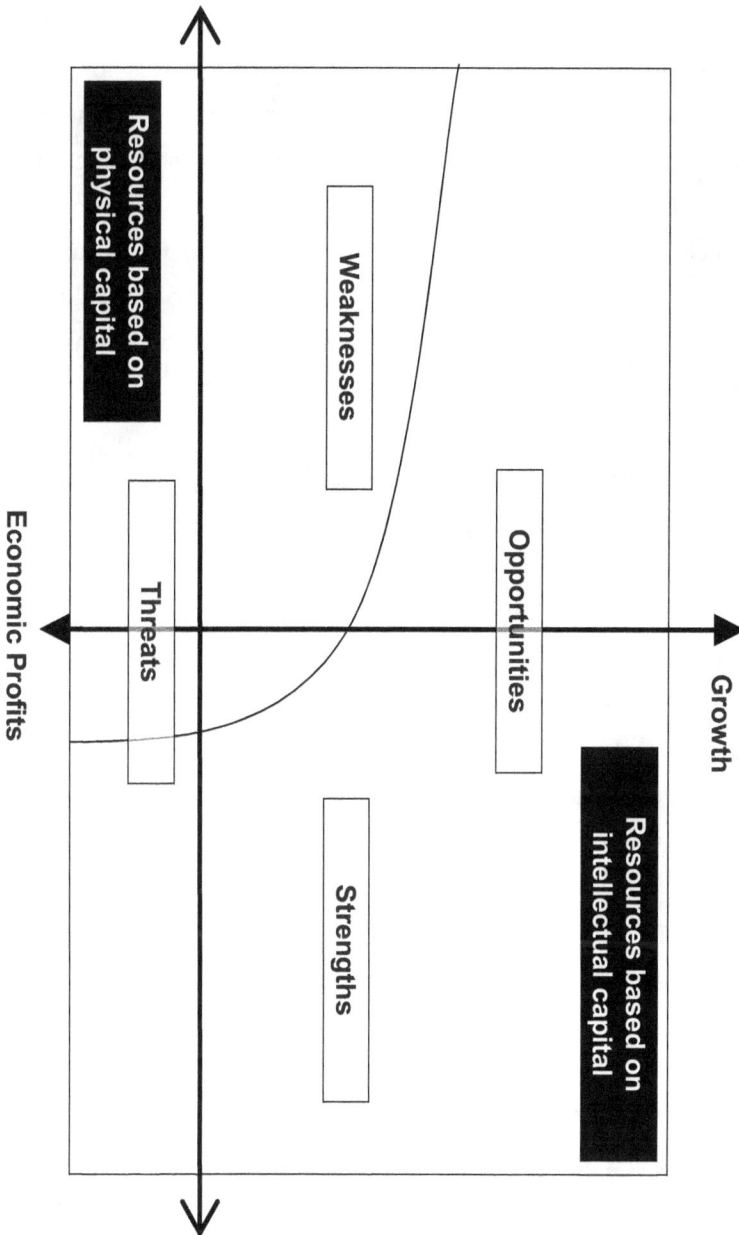

Figure 43. SWOT and economic value creation.

Competitiveness helps organizations to be profitable based on their unique resources. Strengths and weaknesses can be analyzed by comparing the value chains of all competitors to assess how well they meet customer expectations and their competitiveness. These comparisons generate positioning charts, widely used in marketing, to assess how customers perceive the attributes of companies, what prices they can charge, and, consequently, their economic benefits as an indicator of competitiveness. Unique resources are the backbone of value chains; they influence the success of positioning strategies and, consequently, their economic benefits.

- **Opportunities and threats. Their link with growth, innovation, and resource strategies.**

Also, within the SWOT analysis framework, determining opportunities and threats helps assess growth potential. Opportunities or threats are based on how the company's resources help it grow and how external factors such as the economy, politics, financial situation, technology, demand, and competition can transform into something valuable for the company.

The PESTLE (Political, Economic, Social, Technological, Legal, Environmental). Critical thinking.

The PESTLE model is somehow part of the opportunities and threats of the SWOT model. The PESTLE helps analyze the actors and factors arising from the external environment, which allows the company to identify its opportunities or threats and, based on this, to conclude whether it can grow.

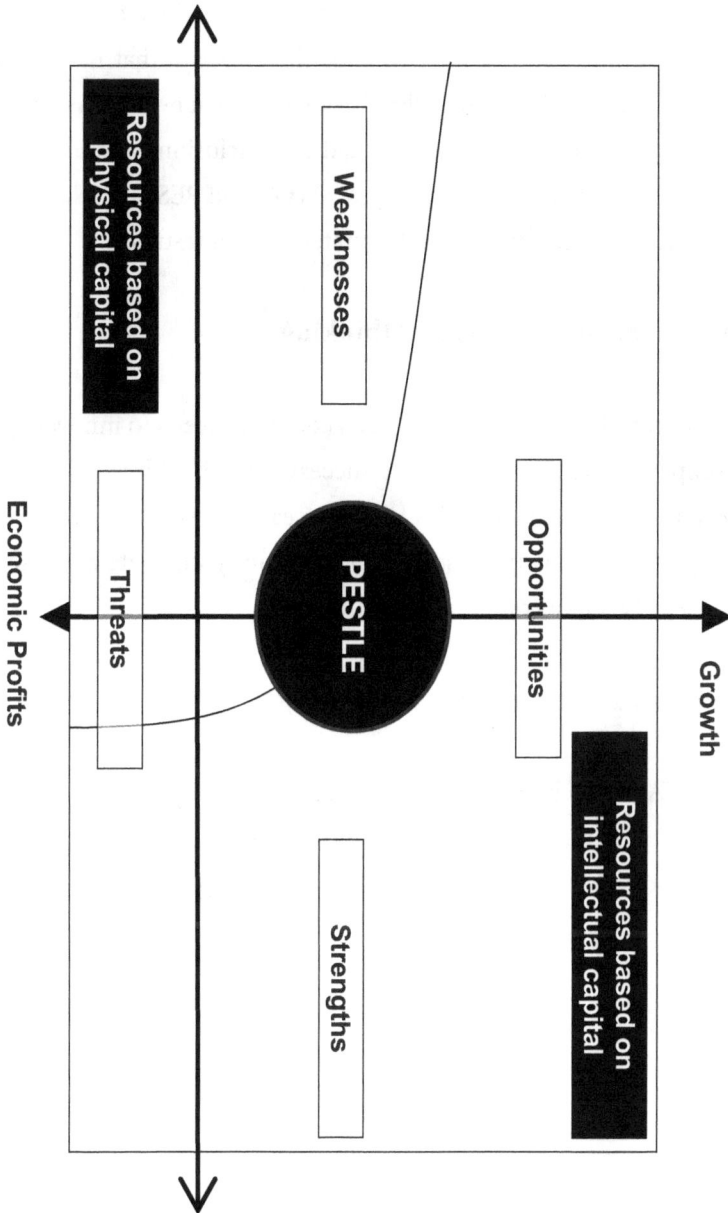

Figure 44. PESTEL and economic value creation.

The introduction of the EVA model helps to visualize that both the SWOT and PESTLE models are resource-based and help to define competitive and innovation strategies. This ends the criticism that many practitioners write useless SWOT and PESTLE analyses that become an accumulation of information, which do not lead to conclusions and are disconnected from an organization's strategies. SWOT and PESTLE relate to economic value creation, environments, strategies, and results.

Blue Ocean Strategies. Critical thinking.

Blue ocean strategies consider that a company needs to innovate to reduce competition and have sustained success. Thus, it addresses both competitive and innovation strategies. A blue ocean strategy only makes sense if the organization has the resources to constantly innovate and use that innovative power as a competitive tool.

The industry life cycle. Critical thinking.

The EVA model helps analyze the industries' life cycle, which depends on the environment, strategies, and results. It constitutes a source of critical and interdisciplinary thinking, integrating and simplifying strategic management.

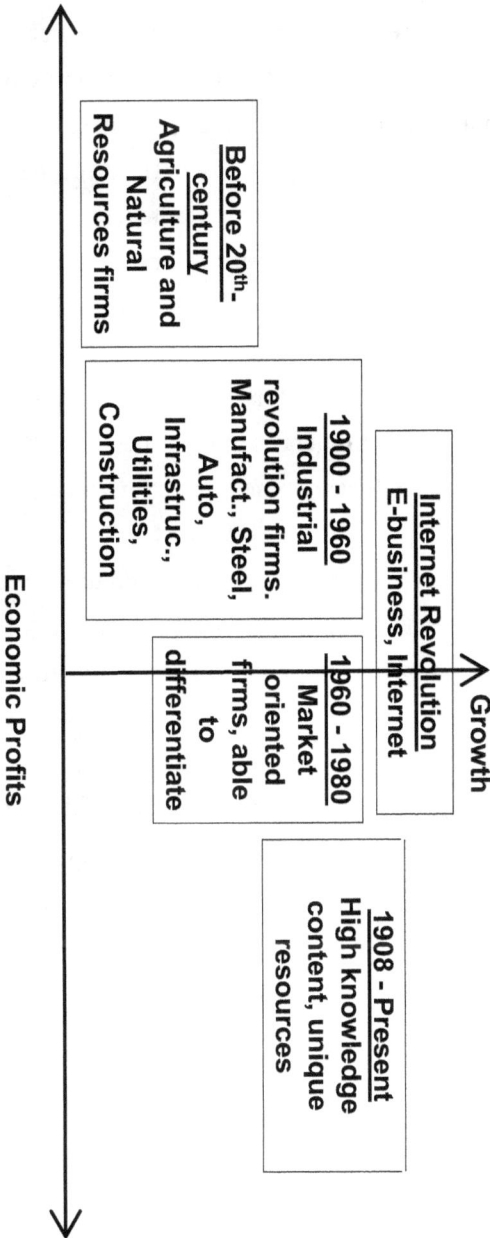

Figure 45. The life cycle of industries and economic value creation.

On the left of Figure 45, with negative economic benefits and low growth, the first group reflects industries that existed before the 20th century and have become mature industries. High competition has transformed their products into *commodities* and standard products and made their prices similar to their marginal costs. Their competitive strategy is low-cost, and their capacity for growth is limited.

The second group (1900-1960) reflects large factories with significant physical capital and low capacity for differentiation, which generates their low economic profits.

The third group (1960-1980) reflects market-oriented companies. Modern marketing greatly influences their strategies, with economic benefits close to 0% because they are based on actions and are easily imitated by competitors.

The next group, located on the right side of Figure 45, represents companies with unique resources, high intellectual capital, high market power, or the ability to collude with competitors. Their uniqueness allows them to have good economic profits.

The industry group at the top of the chart is heavily impacted by the new economy. Although growing rapidly, not all of them can create economic value due to high levels of competition and low capacity for differentiation.

The BCG portfolio matrix. Critical thinking.

The Boston Consulting Group proposed a portfolio matrix to define diversification strategies.

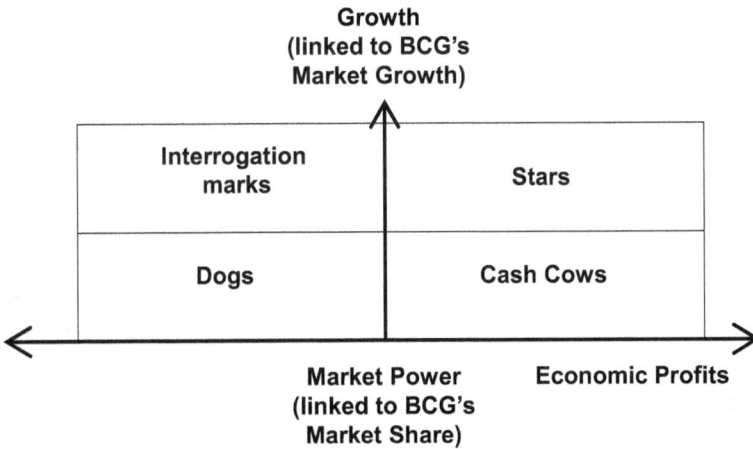

Figure 46. BCG portfolio matrix and economic value creation.

Framing it in the EVA model allows us to visualize other dimensions.

Looking at the graph's horizontal dimension, the BCG matrix's market share is a component of market power.

Looking at the vertical dimension of the chart, market growth provides information about the market's attractiveness. However, it does not say much about the company's competitive position or growth, which are the key factors to consider.

Based on the EVA model, the BCG matrix proposes investment, holding, and divestment strategies, which can be linked to competitive, innovation, resource, organizational, and functional strategies. The EVA model goes further and links these strategies to economic value creation.

The GE/McKinsey portfolio matrix. Critical thinking.

To define a diversification strategy, the GE/McKinsey portfolio matrix analyzes two dimensions: sector attractiveness and competitive position.

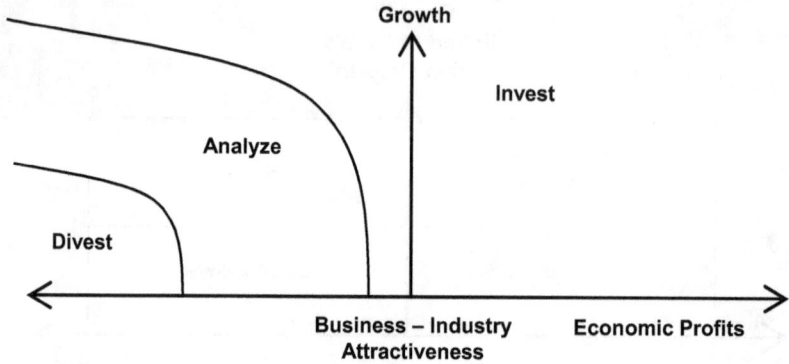

Figure 47. The GE/McKinsey matrix and economic value creation.

The factors that help define industry attractiveness (market size, market growth, profit margin, competitive intensity, technological requirements, vulnerability to inflation, energy requirements, environmental impact, and socio-political-legal environments) and the factors that help analyze competitive position (market share, share growth, product quality, brand reputation, distribution network, promotional effectiveness, production capacity, production efficiency, unit costs, material supplies, R&D performance and management personnel), while valid, do not adequately address the main driver of profitability (the resources that provide market power), and the main driver of growth (the resources to innovate).

The EVA model provides a framework for analyzing these factors; it goes beyond investment-disinvestment recommendations by linking all strategies to economic value creation.

Miles and Snow's typology. Critical thinking.

Miles and Snow analyzed different strategies and organizations and standardized their findings into four types.

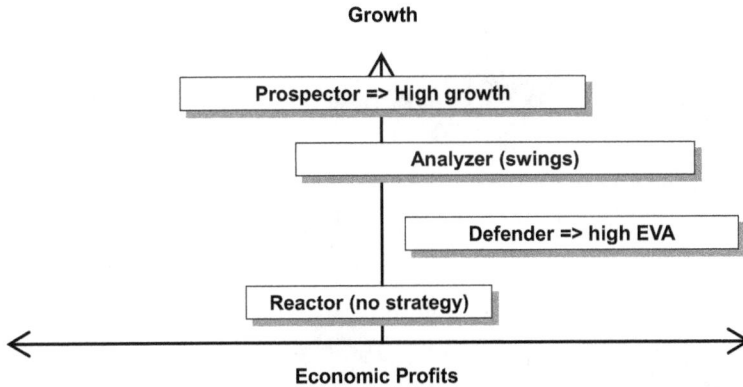

Figure 48. Miles and Snow's typology and economic value creation.

Organizations that fall into the "defender" category create a niche to survive attacks. They use a monopolistic strategy that leads to high economic profits. On the other hand, those of the "explorer" type are oriented towards innovation and diversification, trying to identify and exploit new products and market opportunities. They use innovation strategies, which lead to high growth. Organizations of the "analyzer" type operate between the defender and the explorer. Finally, those responding to the "reactive" type adjust to the environment without strategy.

The EVA model allows Miles and Snow's four typologies to be linked to economic value creation, competitive strategies, innovation strategies, organizational strategies, and functional strategies.

www.ingramcontent.com/pod-product-compliance
Lightning Source LLC
Chambersburg PA
CBHW050505210326
41521CB00011B/2328